Words Matter

The Publisher gratefully acknowledges the generous support of Gordon E. and Betty I. Moore, Marjorie Randolph, and Jamie Rosenthal Wolf, David Wolf, Rick Rosenthal, and Nancy Stephens/The Rosenthal Family Foundation as members of the Publisher's Circle of the University of California Press Foundation.

Words Matter

COMMUNICATING EFFECTIVELY IN THE
NEW GLOBAL OFFICE

Elizabeth Keating and
Sirkka L. Jarvenpaa

UNIVERSITY OF CALIFORNIA PRESS

University of California Press, one of the most distinguished university presses in the United States, enriches lives around the world by advancing scholarship in the humanities, social sciences, and natural sciences. Its activities are supported by the UC Press Foundation and by philanthropic contributions from individuals and institutions. For more information, visit www.ucpress.edu.

University of California Press
Oakland, California

Library of Congress Cataloging-in-Publication Data

Names: Keating, Elizabeth Lillian, author. | Jarvenpaa, S. L. (Sirkka L.), author.
Title: Words matter : communicating effectively in the new global office / Elizabeth Keating and Sirkka L. Jarvenpaa.
Description: Oakland, California : University of California Press, [2016] | Includes bibliographical references and index.
Identifiers: LCCN 2016023975 (print) | LCCN 2016025169 (ebook) | ISBN 9780520291379 (cloth : alk. paper) | ISBN 9780520965171 (e-edition)
Subjects: LCSH: Business communication.
Classification: LCC HF5718 .K43 2016 (print) | LCC HF5718 (ebook) | DDC 658.4/5—dc23
LC record available at https://lccn.loc.gov/2016023975

Manufactured in the United States of America

25 24 23 22 21 20 19 18 17 16
10 9 8 7 6 5 4 3 2 1

to Allan
and
to Mari

Contents

Acknowledgments

We are extremely grateful to the engineers who helped us with this study. Without them it would not have been possible to write this book. (Confidentiality agreements and university rules about research on human subjects prevent us from acknowledging them personally here, but we have them in our thoughts.) We also thank our colleague John Taylor, with whom we initially collaborated on the project on intercultural knowledge systems dynamics. We thank the National Science Foundation for funding the project that led ultimately to this book, written for the engineers we worked with and others like them. We thank our wonderful editor at UC Press, Reed Malcolm, and the enthusiastic anonymous reviewers for the press whose comments enriched the book.

There are many people who helped us along the way. We would like to expressly acknowledge the student research assistants (some of whom are now professionals) who assisted with the project at various stages: Anindita Chatterjee, Melissa Di Marco, Zuhair Khan, Yongsuk Kim, Inger Mey, Nilesh Nayak, Justine Pak, Tanya Raybourn, and Chiho Sunakawa Inoue. We also thank our supportive departments and colleagues at the University of Texas at Austin and our colleagues in other parts of the world who invited us to talk about our findings. We would like to express our appreciation to our students at the University of Texas at Austin for their continued inspiration, and to the many linguistic anthropologists, sociolinguists, and business and communication scholars whose work contributed to our thinking and to this book.

We would like to express appreciation for the opportunity to present some of our research findings and get valuable feedback from several workshops and small conferences. Our thanks to Sangeeta Bagga-Gupta, AaseLyngvær Hansen and participants at the Revisiting Identity Conference in Örebro, Sweden; Åsa Mäkitalo and participants at the Learning and Media Technology Studio, Gothenburg, Sweden; colleagues at the Freiburg Institute for Advanced Studies, Freiburg, Germany; Jacob Buur and his colleagues at the Mads Clausen Institute for Product Innovation in Denmark; Lauren Filliettaz and participants at the Applied Linguistics and Professional Practice conference in Geneva; Jürgen Streeck, Christian Meyer, J. Scott Jordan, and participants in the international workshop on the senses in interaction; Christian Meyer and colleagues at the Center for Global Cooperation Research at the University of Duisberg, Germany; and Mayumi Bono and her colleagues at the National Institute of Informatics, Tokyo.

Others who deserve special thanks for their inspiration and encouragement include Peter Auer, Megan Crowhurst, Adriana Dingman, Alessandro Duranti, Maria Egbert, Melissa Ossian, Juan and Lesley Rodriquez, Marja-Leena Sorjonen, Karla Steffen, Jurgen Streeck, Jonathan Tamez, Deborah Tannen, Susanne Uhmann, Keith Walters, and Sam Wilson. For generous help with cultural details and perspectives, sincere thanks to Saikat Maitra, Marko Monteiro, Alexandra Teodorescu, and Ani Vasudevan. For many conversations about global English and communication in professional environments, thanks to Anna Lindström and Lorenza Mondada. Any errors or omissions are of course our own responsibility.

Elizabeth would like to express her appreciation for a fellowship at the Freiburg Institute for Advanced Studies in Germany, which made it possible to write the first draft—a crucial step for any book. To her husband, Allan, for his tremendous support during the writing of the book, including sharing his perspective as a global professional, she dedicates this book. Sirkka is dedicating the book to her daughter, Marika Gherardi, who began her global travels at the age of three months and has truly become a world citizen.

Introduction

The scorching sun has already set in Kolkata, leaving the Hooghly River in darkness, and most Bengalis have left work long ago. But Arjun, an engineer at a specialized engineering design company, is still on the phone with American engineers, who are just getting to work in Houston, where the time is eleven and a half hours earlier. Arjun stares out at the Hooghly River delta and the lights of homes and cars. He has a one-and-a-half-hour commute ahead of him in nightmarish traffic, and he knows his wife doesn't like to eat dinner until he gets there. His engineer colleagues sitting around the table with him—Rajesh, Akhil, and Gaurav—have shorter commutes. But their families are also being impacted by their global engineering office, which spans time zones and jumps geographic borders.

The American engineers in Texas are energized from coffee, joking through their usual round of morning greetings, asides, and good-natured teasing that Arjun and his Indian colleagues can't see and can barely hear. Arjun says, "Good morning, everyone."

Don replies quickly, "G'morning," and everyone chimes in. But then he realizes he's wrong. "Afternoon!" he says.

Jim corrects him: "Or evening."

"Evening," Don says, somewhat embarrassed.

The American engineers aren't thinking about what time it is in Kolkata. They're reacting from habit, as you can see. They aren't in sync. They realize they have to fix the situation, and too late they realize it's evening in India, but they may not remember how very late in the evening it is there. After a long discussion of some changes the client wants on a design, Don and Jim ask Arjun, Rajesh, Akhil, and Gaurav if they have any questions. Because the line goes quiet, the Americans assume there are no questions, wrap up the meeting, and say their good-byes. (They have a long work day ahead of them; the conversation is just the beginning of it.) In Kolkata, the Indians start their commutes home.

Yet in the following days, the emails that go back and forth make clear that the Indians *did* have some questions but didn't ask them. And because they didn't ask them, they didn't receive crucial information. The Americans worked with the wrong understanding of the Indians' situation for several days. Time was lost. Now the engineers who needed the Indian designs in order to be able work on their part of the project are sitting idle, and the client has been on the phone, angry at the delay, demanding an account and threatening penalty costs. Who will pay for this?

When incidents like this arise, culture and history become visible. In this case, the unique cultures and the histories of West Bengal, India, and the southern United States play a part in the delay. Rajesh told us, "We were ruled by the British for two hundred years," he began, then paused. "So to ask a question to an outsider or to a foreigner is not a very good habit to us. It is a problem. Yes, definitely, it's a problem." The idea of saving questions for later (raising them "behind closed doors," as Arjun referred to it) had caused communication problems that to Don and Jim were avoidable; asking questions for them is routine, even a way to show how smart they are. Weeks later, lingering irritations remained on each side over the other's communication habits. Each side felt the other had breached the correct way for human beings to interact and preserve harmony. The Americans still didn't get that it was evening over there when it was morning for them. And at the start of phone calls, they still wished the Indians "G'morning."

Scene 2

João, who has lived in Rio de Janeiro all his life, is now collaborating with an international engineering team, mostly American engineers from an American firm. He has always sought opportunities to work with people from other cultures, even though his friends wonder why he doesn't work for the national Brazilian oil company. Everybody knows it's a great place for engineers to advance and gain experience.

At the office, Brazilian employees spend a lot of time developing relationships, and João has made many efforts to get to know his American colleagues. It's hard to get to know them virtually, but the Americans don't make it easy, either. Many of them seem to react to friendly chat as if it's a time waster, as if there's a clock ticking to which the Americans are like slaves to a master. João constantly tried to get them to loosen up and enjoy.

One weekend he got married—a huge wedding attended by many family members and guests. There was samba dancing, which João excelled at, and tasty Brazilian food specialties like the sweet *bem casados* that are customary at marriages. When João returned to work, with stories to tell and photos to share, the American engineering manager didn't ask him how the wedding was. João felt so disrespected by this behavior that he started to look for another job, and after a few months he left the project. When he announced he was quitting, the Brazilians in the office sympathized. Several had already told us that the Americans, through their communication behavior, showed they "don't care about people, they are cold and impersonal." For João, the matter of communication was a moral one. Was he not a human being in their eyes? He also worried about what might happen if a family emergency arose; would the company be understanding, or would he lose his job?

Scene 3

Dave and Constantin, two engineers, have started to raise their voices at either end of the line, and everyone has gone quiet around the conference table in the United States, staring at the telecommunication device that is their link to Romania. The day is just beginning for the Americans; Dave and the other Americans are in the office early, at 8:15 A.M., while in Romania, Constantin and his team are ready to wrap up their day.

Dave is upset that the latest calculations uploaded to the computer model don't reflect what they all agreed to on last week's call. The engineers are designing a complex processing plant, and because the client has requested an equipment change, the pressure calculations for the flow of crude oil through the network of pipes have to be changed. But the changes aren't on the model. What happened? Dave knows that his Romanian colleagues like Constantin think Americans are guilty of overengineering things, which his colleagues say wastes money. The Romanians are more comfortable relying on professional engineering tables, which was part of their university training. The pressure calculations have been a source of professional conflict before. Just as Dave has made the case again to Constantin and the Romanian engineers, and the topic is winding down, Constantin says, "We'll see."

Dave hasn't expected any pushback, since the plant will be built for U.S. clients, so his voice registers his surprise. In an angry tone he says, "Did you say, 'We'll see'?"

Because Constantin and Dave didn't learn English in the same cultural context (and it's not Constantin's first language but rather his fourth, after Romanian, French, and Russian), they each interpret the meaning of "We'll see" differently. Constantin likely doesn't realize the cultural buttons he's pushed for Dave by replying in that way. To Dave (and to most American English speakers), "We'll see" is something a parent says to dismiss a child's request. Constantin's Romanian-influenced English intonation pattern has also made his remark seem more final than he probably intended.[1]

"Yes, I said, 'We'll see,' because we shall amend the model," Constantin replies louder this time, for clarity. "Monday you will receive a snapshot of this."

Dave says nothing and moves on to the next item on the agenda.

·　　·　　·　　·　　·

As we researched this book, we sat in on many cross-continental meetings, the kind of meetings now possible with communication technology.

Over and over we witnessed communication breakdowns stemming from different cultural habits and leading to ruined expectations. Just as detrimental as the communication breakdowns themselves was the way the engineers often misattributed what caused them. They sometimes assumed that what was really just a different style of communicating was instead a case of intended rudeness. We saw talented people get fed up with what they felt was continual disrespect, and we watched them quit the project or the company.

There's an irony here: people have enthusiastically embraced the contact and collaboration that digital technologies have made possible. People have promoted these technologies as ways to link offices and save money, grow opportunity, and use expertise wherever it exists on the planet. Whatever the short-term gains of this approach might be, though, communication problems are eroding the long-term gains so severely that these problems need to be addressed. In 2013, the Project Management Institute (PMI) asked over seven hundred project managers and over two hundred business owners to report on the impact of cross-cultural communication failures. The PMI study found that one out of every five projects is unsuccessful due to ineffective communications. And this translated to an estimated $75 million at risk for every $1 billion spent.[2] Arjun, the Indian engineer we mentioned in scene 1, told us that the communication problems between the Indian and American parts of the engineering team at one point stopped the project cold. If the Americans didn't figure out how to do better, "it will always be like us versus them," he said. "Us versus them with a wall in between, that's no good."

Anyone who has worked on a cross-cultural team or managed a global team where face-to-face meetings rarely take place probably finds the opening three scenes familiar, perhaps painfully so, and could contribute anecdotes of their own. Anyone who has worked in a global team setting has likely witnessed firsthand how communication problems are much more than inconveniences. Wherever we encountered them in our research, communication problems were damaging and costly.

In this book, we take a seat next to you and tell you what we learned from the engineers—global professionals like yourself—about cross-cultural communication. We combine what the engineers taught us with what we know from our many years of researching in anthropology, linguistics, communication, virtual teams, and business management. We've also added what many other researchers have learned and observed. We describe a new model that we created based on this input, a model we call the *Communication Plus* model. It's designed to link theory and practice, to give new insights into cross-cultural communication for those already in the work world or about to enter a virtual global office scene. We want you to communicate better in cross-cultural settings, whether a multi-time-zone conference call or a face-to-face meeting, a design review about an innovative technology or a needs-list negotiation. Our model is based on our research on four continents in settings similar to your own. Our Communication Plus model consists of five principles that you can learn and put to work immediately.

In our research, we gathered stories from teams that had to accomplish a complex task in planning and designing—in this case, a state-of-the-art petroleum-processing plant. Our research project, which involved the engineers in four countries, was funded by the National Science Foundation.[3] We questioned why engineers working on complex technical tasks on global teams were reporting that they were not nearly as successful as they thought they would be.[4] This book is in large part possible due to these engineers' generosity in sharing their experiences with us and letting us hang out with them.

The designers we studied were being pulled in different directions. The processing plant they were designing was simultaneously a local project, executed within local rules (which the engineers all knew well), and a high-stakes global project (in which the rules were unclear and had to be negotiated), where mistakes were expensive.

We followed the engineers over a three-year period. In each place and culture, we saw engineers doing their best to manage teamwork in a technologically mediated global workplace. Everywhere, we saw and heard frustration: "I don't get it. Why don't they simply understand what to do!"; "They have no idea what kind of people we are!" Unexpected mistakes were destroying budgets and tempers.

The miscommunication we witnessed and heard about inadvertently poisoned those very relationships and reciprocities necessary to building trust. Since trust is a key ingredient in the success of teams, this was a serious situation. Whether an engineer was from India, Romania, Brazil, or the United States, they told us heartfelt stories about being treated with a lack of respect or hostile intentions, or being frustrated by perceived passive-aggressive behavior.

One of the best engineers, who was an excellent English speaker, quit the project because he could no longer stand what he called the aggressive tone of the Americans' emails. Other Romanian engineers, who sympathized with him, said the American style of communicating made them feel insignificant. After all, the Americans never inquired about them personally or about their families. And when the Romanians tried to establish a relationship, the Americans started in with details of the work ahead of them. "What are we to them, cattle at the market?" the Romanians asked us. Meanwhile, on their side, the Americans felt that they were respecting people by saving their own and the others' valuable time by getting right to the point and focusing on the work at hand. If the Americans mentioned this to the Romanians, it cemented the Romanian view that only time and money, and not people, matter to Americans. These people realized that their bad feelings were generated by different ways and different cultures, but they didn't know how to address these root causes.

Just as detrimental as the communication breakdowns themselves was the tendency to attach bad intentions to the breakdowns, which had actually been caused by unshared assumptions. You saw that play out already in the first three scenes of this book. Even more alarming than the communication failures was the ease of considering a person (whether American, Indian, Romanian, or Brazilian) to be not merely impolite or a poor communicator but someone who was hostile, uncooperative, and even lacking in moral character.[5] Such misattributions, if not corrected, made improving the interactions and repairing the relationships nearly impossible.

COMMUNICATION PLUS

With more attention to communication, a cross-cultural work environment can actually be exhilarating and challenging. You can get opportunities for a new awareness of your own language and culture. You can also get firsthand knowledge of the astonishing diversity of human society that's now linked through technology. Working cross-culturally can be a brilliant, rewarding career move. Learning principles of cross-cultural communication can result in new professional and leadership opportunities. However, when differences in habits of communication aren't recognized, those who are working together on global teams may not be successful.

One of the engineers' problems arose because they didn't share the same office, so they had few chances to observe and informally learn about each other. At first this didn't trouble them because they thought that culture doesn't really matter that much when everyone speaks English. Everyone shared the same professional background, they thought. "An engineer is an engineer," said Joe, one of the American engineers. He added that collaborating globally on engineering projects should be no big deal. As the global project wore on, however, he realized he'd been short-sighted about what's universal about engineering. Culture became very relevant. The engineers told us they wanted information about culture, and they needed it right away.

It's common to find, as we did, that culture is mistakenly seen as just a side issue for global teams until problems develop, calls or emails aren't returned, and cycles of blame have begun. Or until what one engineer called "lightning storms" of conflict arise—sudden, unexpected clashes where cultural histories and expectations are suddenly illuminated, but everyone is still left in the dark.

Executives in many global industries have recognized that differences in communication styles around the world are their thorniest problem. When executives were asked to identify the main factor in problems between cross-cultural teams, most (over 75 percent) listed communication styles.[6] To the engineers we studied, this meant that things "got lost in translation," with "gaps" in understanding. It was their responsibility to get the job done, but they worried that things were "running wide open." When we listened to their stories of miscommunication, we realized that despite being accomplished engineers with excellent problem-solving skills and computational virtuosity, they had ideas about using language and what people do when they communicate that were out-of-date and inaccurate for the global office. They'd been told there wasn't much they could do about communication problems. Experienced colleagues, for example, advised them never to "take it as a given" that people in other countries "understand what you really mean." "How do you know they understand you?" we asked an American engineer. "You don't," he said.

But we believe everyone can learn the skills to continually foster understanding. A premise of this book is that it's impossible to expect others to adapt to our cultural style of communication, because it's difficult for anyone to be completely aware of how much their own culture influences communication. But it is possible to learn key, common principles that underlie *all* human communication systems and every communication act (based on extensive, verified research). And it's possible to put that knowledge to work in every conversation, and to keep polishing one's skills—for example, understanding cultural reasons behind a "failure" to speak directly, or learning cultural reasons behind a "failure" to speak *in*directly.

It's true that the engineers we worked with spent a lot of time discussing many aspects of engineering design, but they rarely spent any time discussing the complexities of how people design communication. This book opens that discussion. Lack of knowledge about how people design, use, and understand language can be just as fatal as a lack of understanding of the soil on top of which a brilliant engineering design will rest. It leads to the wrong predictions and then frustrates problem-solving strategies. As a Romanian engineer said, "Almost anyone can be a good engineer, but if he or she cares about communication—then he or she will move ahead." This engineer was being too modest about his own professional capabilities, but he realized that math and physics weren't enough.

It's a cliché to say that the world is becoming smaller. But it's also a fact that has an impact on the working lives of global professionals. You're likely to work with people who don't share your ideas about creativity or what makes a good design, who don't share your ideas of justice, who understand the causes of psychological stress very differently, who speak a sort of English that's influenced by their first language. In this book, we provide critical communication skills you need in a rapidly changing work world. It's not the special few who do this well. Everyone who does it well had to learn it at some point.

.   .   .   .   .

Our model about the power of language to make or break work relationships in the global office is the Communication Plus model. It's applicable to many settings, not just engineering. It's made up of five principles:

1) seeing language as action, 2) treating the hearer as the key to successful communication, 3) recognizing the importance of building common ground, 4) seeing language as social and cultural, and 5) recognizing the ways in which technology can actually handicap communication.

The first step is the recognition that there's no neutral form of communication and no aspect of communication that's free of culture's influence. Yet in the digital work spaces people inhabit every day, they don't get much information about the culture of the people sharing their desktop from across the world. Without that information, and with the standardization of technological interfaces, it's easy to assume too much similarity. What we say and what they say, how we listen and how they listen, even what we expect from communication itself—all are shaped by unique cultural backgrounds. At one level, this is an admirable aspect of our humanity. At another level, it can easily lead to conflict. Internally, homegrown terms and habits that every professional uses are very efficient. They seem direct and unambiguous. But when communications go global and no one bothers to explain the homegrown terms and habits because the assumption is that they're clear, all sorts of problems can arise. And if the only interactions are through digital spaces, people can't learn things by observing what goes on in the office halfway around the world, or see the real life cycle of a design.

Decisions to collaborate with others internationally are often made by upper management, with little input from the people who have to get the work done. In the management teams on the four continents where our study took place, the idea persisted that with the right planning in one country, a job could be "thrown over the fence" (as they put it) to another country. What was required would be obvious (or so the managers maintained), and employees could figure things out. However, for the engineers, things that "started off in sync" quickly diverged. They learned that, whereas they had relied on many nonverbal cues and opportunities to observe, teach, and learn when working among themselves, these weren't available when their teammates were no longer a cubicle away. We hope this book will help you compensate for those lost opportunities for informal learning.

The revolutionary technology that now makes it possible to work with colleagues across the globe—email, phones, the Internet—requires good communication skills. Adapting communication to new tools is what makes humans excel. Adapting to new cultural environments can also be a source of excellence and innovation.

We are an anthropologist and a business administration expert, and we're both fascinated by the way digital technologies are reshaping culture contact and work. We joined our expertise in culture and communication and in the special challenges of the global business setting for this project. It's true that business and anthropology have different goals in studying human behavior and different ways of studying organizational systems. But combining these fields yields many useful, interesting insights into communication in the cross-cultural, technologically mediated workplace. Our collaboration gave us new insights into our own discipline and cultural differences, too.

This book gives a linguistic anthropologist's view of the importance of conversation in creating our worlds, and the realization that the interpretation of someone else's words is deeply entrenched in cultural habits. It also gives a view on how the very technology that enriches our communication possibilities—email, phones, the Internet, computer modeling software— can be better used if it includes knowledge of how culture influences communication. Language and culture affect everything people do. Rather than try to neutralize culture or pretend that the differences between "us" and "them" are negligible, we built the Communication Plus model specifically with culture in mind.

For the model, we combine a set of principles that anyone can learn and apply in multiple situations without anyone having to give up what their own cultural background says is right and wrong about communicating. Our goal is to enable people to better understand how communication really works and to empower them to gain a research-based understanding of cross-cultural communication. This in turn will lead to better thinking and reacting skills within a multicultural framework.

There are many excellent books on communication that have shown the ways people use language in encounters every day to "get the job done." Here, we take that a step further and talk about getting the job done when there is no shared office, no shared lunchroom or even lunch ingredients, and where forms of eating, relaxing, making friends, and conversing are different, and one doesn't know who might be there in the room on a conference call.

The global work space necessitates speaking one or more common languages. In this book we will use examples of problems when the common language is English. Good communication in English or any other language is not only a matter of getting the grammar right. It's a matter of knowing how to express difficult things, such as a complaint or a dissatisfaction, or even a question, without creating problems in a working relationship.

We believe the only way that the engineers—who were sometimes irritated and exasperated with each other—worked successfully together was when they put into action two ideas. The first idea is that key aspects of cultural *context* are "missing" or unavailable to them because of the technologically mediated settings and lack of face-to-face interaction. We saw engineers (and other communicators) succeed when they recognized this gap and took steps to prevent its negative consequences. The second idea is that all of us are "missing" some cultural *knowledge* in a cross-cultural encounter because of different cultural backgrounds. Engineers (and other communicators) succeeded when they recognized this additional gap and also tried to prevent its consequences. The Communication Plus model is built to provide what's missing, based in large part on what the most successful engineers did.

The successful engineers realized that their sincerity or good intentions were not enough.[7] No matter how technically skilled people are, they still can't solve their communication problems on their own if they believe that good communication comes naturally out of sincerity or good intentions. And communication skills based on research are not taught in engineering schools. But we believe that no matter what a person's background is, they can learn about how culture affects communication skills. After all, if culture helps to shape communication, that means that communication isn't innate. We each had to learn how to communicate in our native language, and we can learn to do it in a second language—and in global languages, too, when technology enables us to reach out to new communication partners.

It's essential to learn more about culture and communication. We're in an age of massive migrations of groups and individuals. Research and history show that despite the proliferation of McDonalds, the influence of hip-hop art forms, the fact that Americans daily wear a form of clothing they borrowed from India (pajamas, from the Persian word), despite the Internet and mobile phones, cultures continue to diverge. "Microfrontiers of culture"[8] arise even within cultures where constantly shifting boundaries of successive innovation, disputes, and collaboration exist, whether sensemaking is based on money, achievement, luck, or witchcraft. (Making sense of what happens can take many forms.)[9] As global organizations look for ways to succeed economically, they recruit men and women located in countries where living and working conditions are quite varied and people have different ways of making sense of what's going on or what's expected. U.S.-employed engineers are working with engineers who sit in offices across the world simultaneously experiencing day for night or night for day. Unseen peoples' voices now emerge surrounded by freeways in Houston or the foothills of the Carpathian Mountains. Or in modern high-rises in rice fields of the Hooghly River, or a few blocks from the sands of Ipanema.

The global digital office is changing many of the ways in which people work and communicate.[10] Professional and technical staff are the crux of many multinational business and education enterprises. As such, they require a book that is about them and written for them, as well as for the managers who direct them. For more than a decade, professional engineering societies and educational groups have called for "soft skills" training in engineering curricula along with training in technical "hard" skills. This book answers that call.

ABOUT THE AUTHORS

Born in the United States, Elizabeth Keating is a linguistic anthropologist who studies culture and communication and is a professor of anthropology at the University of Texas at Austin. In the 1990s, she did her first fieldwork on a tiny island in the Pacific Ocean called Pohnpei, which is located north of New Guinea and east of the Philippines. This research became her first book. In her subsequent career, she has researched communication and design practice among a collaborative team of engineers, mathematicians, doctors, and programmers who were designing a medical diagnostic tool. She has also researched the impact of new communication technology on deaf families and their interactions with sign language. She has published multiple scholarly articles and book chapters on a range of topics. Her father was an engineer, and one of her brothers is an engineer, so she came to the project with some knowledge of the tribe. Her nonwork passions include running along the river in Austin and traveling to hike in the mountains.

Born in Finland, Sirkka L. Jarvenpaa is a professor of information systems and the James L. Bayless/Rauscher Pierce Refsnes, Inc. Chair in Business Administration at McCombs School of Business at the University of Texas at Austin, where she also directs the Center for Business, Technology, and Law. She studies and writes about virtual organizations and teams as well as global collaborative platforms, and she has published over a hundred scholarly articles, including many seminal and highly cited and read papers on virtual teams. Sirkka was the Finnish Distinguished Professor from 2008 to 2012. She holds three honorary doctorates. She has held visiting appointments at institutions ranging from Harvard Business School and MIT Sloan School in the United States to the University of Melbourne in Australia, Hong Kong University of Science and Technology, and City University of Hong Kong in China. Though she has lived in the United States for many years and traveled to many countries of the world, each year she takes time to enjoy a few weeks at her summer cottage in the countryside of Finland. She also travels the world to the Formula One and Formula E races.

This book would not have been possible without business and cultural perspectives. Sirkka understands the global business environment, the roles of technology in changing the workplace, and how business systems fit together on a local and global scale. Elizabeth brings knowledge of cross-cultural communication and the role of culture in the workplace, as well as knowledge of research on how human interactions are both reflections of culture and sites where new culture is emerging. This book is the product of our unique collaboration.

OUR APPROACH

Because we were interested in learning about the impacts of culture on cross-cultural work teams using virtual spaces, we had to travel to where people are working and talk to them about challenges and successes from their point of view. Funding from the National Science Foundation enabled us to travel to Mumbai and Kolkata in India, to Rio de Janeiro in Brazil, to

Ploieşti and Bucharest in Romania, and to Seattle and Houston in the United States to talk with and observe engineers at work. We sat alongside them in their meetings and at other parts of their day. We had coffee and lunch together. We were there for project kickoffs, weekly updates, and design reviews. We watched engineering and management presentations, we went with the engineers to chili cook-offs and to cricket matches, and we toured Dracula's castle in Transylvania. We went to Brazilian all-you-can eat steakhouses (*churrascarias*). We followed up with individual interviews about what we saw. In all, we spent 400 hours in seven offices, taking over six hundred pages of notes and making 125 hours of recordings. Through interviews we learned about the engineers' backgrounds and attitudes, and we heard their stories about communication situations and how specific problems affected them.

The time we spent among engineers was important for another reason: it helped us account for some stereotypes about their unique professional culture. Some readers may find it interesting that we would choose to study communication among engineers, given their reputation as bad communicators. In one of our first meetings with the engineers, one of them questioned our choice as a study population on this topic. He illustrated what he meant with a joke. "How do you tell an engineer with good social skills?" he asked. We didn't know. "He looks at *your* shoes instead of his shoes." After spending some time with them and learning about their worldview, though, we found that they were excellent research partners. They were analytical, they loved their work, and they were genuinely curious about culture. Perhaps most important, they were aware that, as one of them said, their language could betray them, and they wanted to minimize those threats. We benefited from input from a broad range of engineers, which provided us a privileged view of the challenges that people face on global teams.

Because we traveled to each location, we were able to observe interactions from many sides. This gave us insight into the local business and cultural contexts of these countries and an understanding of how the people talked and thought about them. In response to questions about culture, people often reply that "this is the way we have always done things." But an anthropologist knows that this is a grossly oversimplified phrase that represents centuries of difficult adaptations, while the business expert understands the evolution of the economic systems in which those cultures evolved.

We observed many scenes of daily life as we lived and worked abroad for short periods, whether on public buses going to the office in Romania, or on walks on the Maidan in Kolkata on the weekend, or while eating *feijoada* in Rio de Janeiro. We had many conversations about the different approaches of business and anthropology to culture contact and communication. Business and anthropology have different goals in studying human behavior and organizational systems. Suggesting "best practices" to the people who are being studied, for example, is not a typical approach in anthropology; but in business, it is. Anthropologists rather assume that there is no "best" practice or society or culture, but instead focus on comparing cultures to describe human diversity and try to understand a practice from the native's point of view. Some linguistic anthropologists, however, like business and education researchers, are interested in applying theory and improving work practices in order to minimize misunderstandings and improve communication[11] or opportunity.

Our fieldwork was thrilling. It was also, at times, discouraging. We had to deal with language issues, adaptation issues, power failures, scheduling around people's busy agendas and our own teaching schedules, monsoon rains, environmental challenges, and the challenges of gaining trust. This was coupled with our dependence on people's willingness to talk about topics that might put them in a poor light or paint them as failures. (All of the names we use in the book are pseudonyms, and other identifying features of the projects and firms have been altered.) The engineers and the company managers were all extremely generous with their time and ideas and welcomed us to their worlds. Without their generosity and openness, the project and this book wouldn't have been possible. They were very patient with our questions, follow-up queries, and clarifying requests, and they helped us understand their theories about communication and work. They took time from their high-pressure schedules to help us. They wanted to know more about culture, and they wanted to know it as soon as possible.

Without spending time with the engineers in their own environments, we couldn't have discovered the gap between how one set of engineers thought they were making sense of each other's talk and how the other set of engineers were actually making sense of them (each from their own cultural perspective). Most people's ideas about communication are very culturally specific, but they are also very speaker-centric, focusing on the speaker as the source of communication problems. But it is important to focus on the hearer, too.

We'll give you an example. Akhil, one of the Indian engineers, told us that he couldn't understand 10 to 20 percent of what the Americans said because of the way they pronounced English. When he was in conference-call meetings with ten or fifteen people, he said, he had difficulty understanding at least two or three of the American engineers. It also turned out that for cultural reasons, Akhil wasn't comfortable interrupting the meeting to ask these two or three engineers for clarification. He told us that if he couldn't understand "then and there," he asked other colleagues in India after the meeting was over: "If I don't understand, the person beside me is getting him, so I can get it from him. It's not good to interrupt in between." The problem with this approach is that the others may not be getting it in parts or in whole, and important details may get lost in the gap. If the American engineers had focused more on the hearer as a key player in communication, the problem could have been corrected. We had also attended many conference calls with Akhil, where we noticed that he never asked anyone to repeat or clarify what they'd said, and we were surprised when he told us he was missing so much. Across four cultures, many engineers in multiple companies told us similar stories. All of them helped us build the Communication Plus model, which includes a focus on the hearer.

Traveling to the different local sites allowed us to experience for ourselves the different cultural spaces—the language, music, traffic, sights, odors, tastes, pageantry, laughter, dress. We traveled through the warm, dusty streets of Kolkata after our plane landed at midnight at the Netaji Subhash Chandra Bose Airport. In the back of an old taxi we felt the roads worn by monsoon rains, and we passed communities of glass-walled highrises next to cardboard shacks crowded along the river with plastic sheeting for roofs. But the American engineer we left back in Houston was able to see only the "Send" button, which started a journey he couldn't see as his engineering document traveled to India. The computer screen measures distance only in folders or inboxes. The drawing made in Houston, though, will be interpreted in other countries, in the presence of other histories and lifeways, and these cultural processes will unexpectedly influence the way the document is interpreted and worked with. And engineering work, as one engineer said, "is about the deliverables—drawings, if you will. You know—how many drawings, what are they going to look like, when are you going to issue them."

The work is nowadays also about tracing culture. As with many aspects of communication, members of every culture are largely unaware of how much they understate background information—that is, until something goes wrong. Take the way people arrange themselves in a conversation. In some cultures, people stand quite close to each other when they're talking. In others, people like more distance. When individuals with these different styles of talking try to have a conversation, one of them is always moving closer, and the other is always backing away. The way people automatically embody their culture is usually in the background and might become clear only when they realize they're involved in this awkward dance.

Communication is not as straightforward as people believe it is. And because people believe it's supposed to be straightforward, they try to fix the wrong things. They try to be more "clear and direct." Or they encourage a collaborator to behave in a way that goes against that person's cultural norms, such as advising them to "just say no!" directly. And because people don't understand how deeply embedded culture and language are, they might not understand a person's indignant reaction to their suggestion that the person throw away the lessons that their parents and grandparents taught them about how to behave in the world.

That good communication is direct communication is one of the assumptions we debunk in *Words Matter: Communicating Effectively in the New Global Office*. But it's not the only one. Following are seven others we saw giving engineers trouble.

ASSUMPTIONS THAT CAUSE TROUBLE

- The assumption that in every communication situation one person knows something that the other doesn't (an assumption about *the purpose of communication;* i.e., that if there's no information to convey, there's no point in communicating, since information transfer is the main goal)
- The assumption that all hearers can be treated alike (i.e., the *myth of a universal hearer*)

- The assumption that information is all the same and carries the same force, no matter where it comes from (an assumption about *the value of information*)

- The assumption that if people *speak the same language*, even if some are not native speakers, they ought to understand each other (i.e., meaning is always in what is actually said rather than in what's not said, what's hinted at, or what the person is already expected to know)

- The assumption that communication is based on a set of *clear, rational rules* (and that people can tell you what these are)

- The assumption that a good communicator somehow knows *how much information* to give and how much people need

- The assumption that culture is simply customs and habits and not cognitive; that therefore *the effects of culture can be neutralized* by using the right language or by leaving culture "checked at the door"

- The assumption that just *being direct and clear* will ensure good communication

These assumptions are probably familiar. They're ways people commonly talk about communication. They form a typical communication model. By *model*, we mean a set of general principles based on cause-and-effect relations that people use as a guide to gain control over outcomes. We're not saying that the communication models and assumptions that people like Dave, Constantin, Arjun, and João have are wrong; we're saying that they're mostly insufficient for the digital communication environment in which these engineers live and work.

NEW ASSUMPTIONS FOR BETTER OUTCOMES

The Communication Plus model is a set of communication principles for the global workplace of the twenty-first century. The principles are broad enough to apply to many cross-cultural situations. Sketched briefly, the principles of the Communication Plus model are these:

- Language is action, not information. Language is more about *getting things done in the world* than anything else.[12] What a person does next (or says next) in conversation can tell you a lot about what they thought just happened.[13] People build up understanding piece by piece, through the give-and-take of talk.

- *The hearer is the most important player.*
- For people to have successful interactions, they need to *build common ground* (checking if common "ground" has been established is important in the digitally mediated cross-cultural office).
- *Language is social (and cultural).* By *social,* we mean that in every interaction, language provides its speakers with unique ways to *build, rebuild, or destroy relationships* between people. By *cultural,* we mean that language use is intertwined with important ideas about *what a person is supposed to be* (and how a person is supposed to behave as a moral person) and aesthetic aspects of behavior.
- *Technology is a handicap,* and we must compensate for it.

Arranged around a specific principle of the model, each chapter of this book explains the principle, illustrates it with examples from our observations and other research, and provides practical advice for implementing the principle.

We show how language is action rather than a conduit for information. Once you realize that *speaking is about getting things done in the world* (reminding, criticizing, humoring, inviting, rejecting, recognizing, disagreeing), you'll be more sensitive to the fact that your language actions can be misunderstood if those same actions aren't recognizable actions to others of another culture. If what you do with language doesn't look like what someone from another culture does with language in theirs, there will be misunderstandings.

It's crucial to remember that *mutual understanding proceeds sequentially.* That is, one person says something (does something), and another person responds (does another action) based on that, and so forth. Because many aspects of communication are routine, people become very good at predicting what might be next in a sequence or what might be upcoming or how something might play out. However, in the cross-cultural setting, speakers and hearers can often find their predictions wrong and conversations going in unexpected directions. They can be trained to be more vigilant in monitoring and repairing these sequences.

In the context of the global, technologically mediated office, the hearer is the most important player, and the focus has to be on *getting feedback from hearers* and training them to give the kind of feedback that is taken for granted or expressed nonverbally in face-to-face interactions. A lot of communication training, especially in corporate environments, is aimed at improving the speaker's behavior. The hearer is often a forgotten participant.[14] In cross-cultural settings that take place through technology or are computer-mediated, where many feedback cues are absent, you must remain vigilant about actively collaborating with hearers on meaning and comprehension. Not only is it important to keep the hearer in mind. In the global workplace, it's also necessary to have *accurate ideas about the hearer.*

We'll show how interactions with other people are more successful if the participants build or have built what is called *common ground.* This refers to a shared understanding of the topic and function of the interaction.[15] More than simply rapport, common ground is about both background information and emotions. In a cross-cultural interaction, less common ground can be assumed, and more has to be explicitly provided. On the best engineering teams we saw, the team members were actively and continually building and maintaining common ground with the other team in very simple ways. You will have to be careful not to "oversuppose and undertell."[16] For instance, you might have to say what might be thought obvious. You might have to be redundant. You may have to explicitly ask people if they understand.

We show how *language is essentially social and cultural.*[17] Each interaction with others involves relationship building and maintenance. If there are misunderstandings or relationships are damaged, language also provides resources for repairing these situations. Every culture uses these language resources in unique ways, but there are also big similarities across cultures. For example, one important way in which every culture uses language multiple times a day is in recognizing another person's humanity—including their accomplishments, their dignity, and their special relationship to the speaker.

But ways of recognizing people vary enough to be at times unrecognizable. What seems like a lapse or deliberate disrespect is frequently an effort by someone to do what they think is right. Americans tend to regard relationships in work settings as less hierarchical and more peer-to-peer than do natives of other cultures; for example, in Romania hierarchical relationships are expected. If one culture acknowledges peoples' humanity by each person treating others as peers or kindred spirits, but if in another culture any assumption of being a kindred spirit is considered rude except in limited circumstances, a member of each culture may feel they have not been treated with humanity by a member of the other. Among the engineers, unintentionally disrespecting someone's identity, perhaps through using a way to acknowledge them that they didn't recognize, sometimes caused hurt feelings that affected good relations.

We talk about how *technology reduces the signals and cues* we're used to depending on for communication, and the sorts of adaptations in communication style that must be made for a global office in which technologically mediated communication is the most visible form of context.[18] Good strategies include increased redundancy and increased checking of understanding, even though it's true that these communication styles can also irritate participants.

In each chapter, before explaining our model in detail, we describe and illustrate the typical ideas and assumptions about communication that we found among engineers. At each step, we show how these ideas about communication can damage or limit communications in the digital office. We want to convince you to change some of your ideas about how communication works.

Everyone we spoke with had ideas about how communication works. Not all cultures have the same ideas and prescriptive advice about communication: some cultures expect more disclosure from speakers and hearers, for instance, or have differing degrees of tolerance for ambiguity in conversation. In some cultures it's considered better to be deliberately unclear in order to avoid conflict and to distribute responsibility for outcomes. Any good communication model has to take into account the fact that people want, and perhaps even need, to feel recognized and respected by others. In fact, you'll be surprised at how many communication practices are designed to preserve relationships. Meaning is a product of a dynamic interaction between a speaker and a hearer.

We call our model Communication Plus because we feel that if people add a few key ideas to what they already know about communication, and change a couple of assumptions, they will be more effective. We're not asking readers to give up what they do natively, but we do think their projects and teams would benefit from using this additional model.

1 Communication in the Wild

Let's go back to the American engineering firm after the tense phone call between Dave and Constantin had concluded. Even after four months of collaboration, communication between the two offices was still a problem.

"I don't understand why those guys don't just simply know what to do!" said Jim, one of the American engineers, after the cross-continental meeting had ended.

Another engineer, Bob, remarked that if they could only work together face to face, they wouldn't have these communication problems, and many others nodded. The reality was that traveling to work face to face was too expensive. Maybe an executive or two could go to a distant work site. Not the whole engineering team, though.

Lee, an American engineer, suggested a solution to us when we interviewed him later: "We just need to be more direct and clear."

Direct and clear. It's worth spending some time with Lee's idea. Could the American, Brazilian, Indian, and Romanian engineers understand each other better if they were direct and clear? To an engineer, this sounds plausible.

To many other people, his suggestion might seem reasonable as well. We had heard something similar from engineers in other offices: "Let's make what we say—or write in emails—unambiguous." But we knew enough about communication to be doubtful. Many people think that directness, clarity, and lack of ambiguity make for good communication, and that a good communicator is someone with those traits. But once you dig into this suggestion, you realize that it's not so workable after all. You also might start to see that it's not the only assumption that people hold about communication. In our work, we collected a lot of these assumptions, many of which don't match what people communicating with digital tools in the global workplace need to know about culture and communication.

One red flag that's raised by Lee's suggestion is, Can an utterance really be made "neutral," and can information really stand alone? Lee has assumed that information other than a key message is unnecessary and confuses people. His idea assumes that information can be abstracted out of one context or situation, reorganized clearly, and then delivered concisely and without ambiguity in another.[1] But take the following sentence as an example: Jim asks Dumitru, "Where are those engineering drawings you were going to send me?" What the speaker really means by this sentence doesn't exist anywhere in the sentence. In this case, key information isn't located in the words themselves but rather in the surrounding context as well as in people's memories of other such sentences and how they played out.[2] The speaker is not asking for a precise location of the drawings, but rather is making a complaint that something promised wasn't delivered. A perfectly coherent answer might be: "Oh sorry, I'm running behind." An impudent or joking answer would be the exact location (seemingly) asked for—for example, "Right here on my desk." How can it be that the *coherent* answer is the one that *doesn't* answer "where" but instead answers "why" or even "when"? Isn't "where" what was asked for? And how in the world can the answer to the real content ("where") be impudent?

Lee thinks that a good communicator can create an utterance that's decipherable by any audience if it's clear and direct. We can see that this view looks to be in trouble. It ignores many aspects of the ways that people really communicate with each other, notably the role of context and cultural conventions and habits. In this case, using the question "Where are the drawings?" potentially avoids conflict by using a question about location. The utterance's *intended action* or impact is to get the other person to send the drawing as soon as possible, to express one's disappointment at the unexpected delay, and also to preserve the relationship.

Lee might disagree. As an engineer, he might point out that clarity and directness do matter in technical fields like science and engineering, where engineering knowledge is thought to be easily detached from an engineer and his surrounding culture. Engineers tend to think that mathematical symbols make up a universal language that's culture-independent. While it's true that math symbols are a universal means of communicating certain types of relationships, people who study math education know that culture still has a role to play. For instance, there's no single way to do mathematics procedures like counting, ordering, sorting, measuring, and weighing; each culture has its own procedures. You can see this in something as simple as numerical ordering for the date. In the European system, it's day-month-year (e.g., 20-6-2015), while Americans use month-day-year (6-20-2015). There are dates of the year that can easily be confused with each other if you don't understand which system the numbers stand for. And these number differences were confused by the Americans and the Romanians we studied. After several costly mishaps about delivery dates, they decided to use the word for the day of the month instead of the numeral.

It turns out that technical and professional knowledge is *not easily pulled from its cultural context* after all. Even though the Indian engineers, like the other engineers, considered engineering to be universally understandable because it's "all math," they told us one story that they thought illustrated some communication problems they'd been having. The story was about one American company's confusing way of categorizing drawings. It turns out that the professional knowledge they all shared about engineering design was wrapped in other information they didn't share. The American company used two similar labels for two different stages of a technical document: "issued for comments" and "issued for checking." The Indian engineer explained to us that from his point of view, there was no difference between issuing a drawing for comments and issuing it for checking. In both cases, engineers checked the work and made comments. As he explained, "If you find something that needs to be commented on, you comment." After multiple misunderstandings about how and when to make comments on drawings, the Indians sought clarification from the Americans but didn't get a satisfactory answer. They still got in trouble for doing the wrong thing. Ultimately they figured out on their own that the Americans' terms denoted two different types of drawings in an important sequence. First a drawing was made and issued for comments, then a comment cycle followed, and then the drawing was returned to the design team. Then it was fixed and "issued for checking." Misunderstandings had occurred because the engineers in Kolkata had described a drawing as "issued for checking" when it was really still in the comment stage, and therefore the wrong conclusions were drawn as to how much work had been accomplished or what stage the work was in. Even worse, the credibility of the Indian team had suffered as a result. This may seem like a very minor issue at first glance, but the consequences of this misunderstanding were not minor at all. The Indian team's credibility was damaged, and it took time, lots of analysis, and a number of mishaps before anyone could get to the bottom of the problem.

Internally, home-grown terms like these seem easy to understand. But when the communications go global and no one bothers to explain them because the assumption is that they're obvious, all sorts of problems can arise.[3] And if the only interactions are through digital spaces, people can't learn things by observing what goes on in the office, or see how the terms fit into the real life cycle of a drawing as they see the drawing move around through the different desks in the office.

Another problem with Lee's idea to be direct and clear is that people sometimes withhold critical information deliberately. What results is that important information gets located in what's *not* said. For instance, American engineers who were working with Brazilian engineers told us that they wished the Brazilians would "just say no" instead of avoiding giving negative news, which the Americans thought slowed things down. But from the Brazilians' perspective, they weren't ignoring anyone. Rather, Brazilians have a cultural aversion to directly refusing requests. For them, it felt most correct to refuse indirectly. In a similar way, the Romanian engineers thought the Americans were withholding critical information when they didn't offer feedback. The Americans, on the other hand, tended to assume that when they didn't give any feedback, their collaborators would conclude that everything was okay. After all, if there's no complaint, then the job's been well done. But when we talked to the Indians and Romanians, we found that they experienced the Americans' silence or lack of feedback about the quality of their work as criticism. The result was that the Indians and Romanians thought they were being criticized (because of what was *not* said), when the Americans were actually satisfied with the work. As you might already have guessed, when Americans heard nothing from Indians, Romanians, or Brazilians, the Americans assumed everything was fine. As we demonstrated in the situation in which Arjun and the other Indians were not asking questions, engineers sometimes have very good culturally based reasons for not saying anything, regardless of the positive or negative status of the project. In all cases, these unexpected *interpretations of what isn't said* resulted in costly delays and feelings of being unacknowledged as a human being.

We're not done picking on Lee's suggestion to make communication "clear and direct," because it has another assumption embedded in it. This is the assumption that people in a communicative situation have one of two states: either they have information or they don't. Said another way, this is the assumption that if there's no information to convey, there's no point in communicating. But take the following sentence: "It's cold in here." Or "You're late." Or when Dumitru says, "Yes, but it's Friday afternoon." In these sentences, the speaker isn't really passing along information that the other person doesn't have. Rather, the person is using language to reflect on his or her relationship with another person. The statements are a kind of complaint that the person doesn't feel the relationship is being properly taken care of. The hearer has to infer what's being said (someone should turn the heat up, or I expect an explanation, or should we be expected to work on Saturday). Maybe a topic is being opened for negotiation. All of this reflects how language does "social" work and has social goals; it doesn't just pass information along.

Or take the example in which American engineer Don said to one of the Romanian engineers about the Romanian design, "Just look at it. It looks weird." All the engineers were staring at the same model, even though some were at their desks in a small two-story building on a tree-lined side street in a Romanian town while others were at their desks in humid Houston, beside an eight-lane freeway. By saying, "Just look at it," Don was assuming that the Romanian engineers already knew what a design was supposed to look like. "Just look at it" is a directive to Dumitru and his other colleagues to use information *they already have* about design. The problem is that Dumitru has his own idea of what makes a good design, and the Romanians have used this so-called weird design on other projects before. In these sentences, Don isn't just passing along data or information that he knows to one who doesn't know; he's *trying to get something done:* change a drawing. If you inspect these utterances purely for their informational value (just look at it; it's cold; it's Friday) and not as something intended to produce action in the hearers, you might miss the messages they carry.

One afternoon, the Romanian and American engineers were on a conference call to check a design for a series of pipes that were going to carry crude oil and other fluids in the processing plant. The digital 3-D model was on their screens. The engineers on each continent clustered around the computer monitors, staring at the piping diagrams. The pipes were colored blue, yellow, red, and purple to signify separate stages of design and different functions. In this remarkable scene, both sets of engineers were able to see the same computer model at exactly the same time. However, as we've discussed, assuming that everyone is interpreting what they're looking at in the same way is a mistake. This became most clear when Bob said to Dumitru "Can we make that water line at the top more accessible?"

On the surface, it looked like Bob was seeking information about whether something could be done. But in the way that Bob used English, he was really telling Dumitru to change the water line. What Dumitru may or may not have known is that Americans make directives polite by giving them in the form of a question about ability. If he didn't recognize that, there would undoubtedly be problems with the design process. But maybe he had enough experience with native English speakers to recognize that questions about ability are one of the most favored form of English directives. English speakers say, "Can you open that window?"; "Can you pass the grits and gravy?"; "Can you stop interrupting me?" Children, when they're being mischievous or "naughty" (as the British English and Indian English speakers say), will play around with the form of these directives and reply, "No, I can't [stop interrupting you]." They've merely answered the surface or apparent form of the question (about ability). This has the predictable result of annoying the one who wanted some quiet and had formulated a polite directive to get it.

American directives also often contain the word *we* or *let's* as a way to mitigate the force of ordering someone else to stop what they're doing and pay attention to one's needs. The *let's* is misleading, too. It pretends the action will be collaborative, and that you will do it together. But only Dumitru is being directed to change the water line.

In fact, even though it's true that Dumitru, João, and others you will meet in this book learned English in school or on the job, they won't necessarily be aware that Bob's sentence doesn't mean what it seems to mean.

The indirectness that Americans prefer to use (like when they ask about a person's ability in order to get that person to do something) is difficult for nonnative English speakers to interpret. To American ears, though, nonnative English speakers can seem too direct, impolite, and disrespectful. But that's because nonnative English speakers are used to the grammatical tools of their own native languages, like using pronoun choice to carry respect messages—something we'll get to in a bit.[4]

Let's go back to Lee's suggestion that all communication be "direct and clear" and linger on the notion of directness. Why are people, as one Indian engineer stated, "maddeningly indirect?" (He had been talking about an American engineer.) Some cultures do value directness, but most cultures value indirectness. Boldly directing another person threatens that person's desire to be treated with dignity; it's considered to be a poor way to motivate someone to do things. Over centuries of human collaboration, every culture has devised ways to limit the potential conflict generated by telling someone what to do (and therefore taking away their autonomy).

Thinking about directness gets us back to the common assumption that communication is always about transmitting information. This assumption is bolstered by popular metaphors (in American English, anyway) that encourage the idea that when you communicate there is someone who knows more and someone who knows less. Well-known idioms display the sense that communication is about passing information from a single human brain to another. Metaphors like "Let me see if I can get this idea across to you" and "That went over my head" and "He didn't come across well" all reinforce the notion that information moves from one person over to another in discrete packets, and that these packets can be designed to be understood even if they're taken out of context or sent to someone new. (The underlying metaphor is one of communication as a conduit or pipeline).[5] Lee's suggestion about "clear and direct" communication is rooted solidly in this metaphor. If we keep the conduit between us uncluttered with social interchange, he is saying, then communication will surely be more likely to succeed. The metaphor leads people to assume that communication consists of two separate and independent processes: that of encoding (speaking) and decoding (hearing). People are focusing on packets of information when they say, "It didn't compute" or "The message got lost in the process." But our brains don't work like machines.

This assumption that we've been talking about is damaging because it leads people away from acknowledging that speakers and hearers must work together to produce shared meaning. It also keeps people from recognizing how multiple interpretations are always possible. When the American engineers didn't receive any questions from their Indian counterparts in the phone call in scene 1 of the introduction, they assumed that their message had been decoded successfully. (To quickly reprise, the Americans opened the floor up to questions, but the Indians didn't have any—even though they did. The Americans took the silence for understanding.) This wrong interpretation could have been avoided if the Americans had had a more dynamic communication model, one that might allow them to practice how meanings are negotiated, not merely transferred from one brain to another.

This assumption—*that communication is all about information transfer* —wasn't held by Lee only. Other engineers we spoke with shared it, too. As a result, they focused on message content and clarity when they tried to fix their problems in communication or tried to create an environment for good communication. This didn't help them solve communication problems, though. Why? Because communication isn't solely about transferring information from one who knows to one who doesn't. This might be surprising to some people, who might ask, "Where else could problems in communication lie if not in the speaker's message itself?"

It's tempting to focus on information, but too much focus on information overshadows other aspects of communication in cross-cultural environments that have big implications for getting the job done. Recall the Project Management Institute study that found that one out of every five projects is unsuccessful due to ineffective communications. Part of this is due to the context missing in today's communication technology, and part of it is due to forgetting about the cultural aspect of communication and thinking too much about information only.

The information-transfer idea is found in many books on communication. The concept has its historical roots in the development of the telephone and radio in the early twentieth century. It was also influenced by the cybernetic revolution after World War II, when people were thinking about complex social and even biological organisms as systems of information. Even though the information-transfer model of communication hasn't been around that long, it has a strong foothold in America and other countries in the West. Meanwhile, in other cultures information has different histories. On the island of Pohnpei (where Elizabeth did her first anthropology fieldwork), for example, the information you have contributes to building and maintaining your life force (energy) so directly that giving information to people can damage your well-being.

The information-transfer concept is not so prominent in ideas about communication in other countries, except in some educational settings. In many cultures, a good communicator is a person who is tactful or who is authorized (by their social role) to be the communicator. In others, a good communicator is a person who can say things in a "veiled" or artfully covert way, or in a way that invites multiple versions. Some cultures don't focus on the speaker as a transfer point, but rather on the hearer's role to figure things out. In Japan, a good communicator is described as a hearer who does a kind of participatory guesswork, to fill out the speaker's communication.[6] Some cultures use allegory or a short poem or a pithy, succinct saying to make a crucial point.

You can see that there are other problems with Lee's information-transfer assumptions about communication, like assuming everyone has the same idea about what constitutes information and how freely it should be given out. When unique cultural assumptions are applied globally, some people aren't going to get what's going on. And even though people in North America and Europe talk a lot about information transfer as important in communication, they actually provide a lot of information very indirectly. Or they assume that everyone has a lot of background information that's never referred to directly. In everyday work life, people often show things indirectly through language rather than by directly saying them. People use metaphors and idioms. They try to tell things in a compelling way to keep the hearer focused and engaged, and they use colorful speech and create analogies. Though Westerners might value transfer of information, that's not what they themselves do; they merely talk about communication that way, because that's how their communication model is built. The Communication Plus model instead is built not on how people think about communication, but on how they do it. Communication Plus builds on the ways people are already used to communicating, and adds on five skills. Using the Communication Plus skills makes contradictions like this idea of information transfer more apparent.

THE MYTH OF THE UNIVERSAL HEARER

Perhaps the most dangerous assumption in Lee's recommendation to be clear and direct is this: when an engineer thinks that the main goal of communication is producing a clear sentence, either in speech or in writing, they are employing another piece of their communication model: the *myth of the universal hearer*. In this view, every hearer is similar. In reality, however, all hearers aren't the same. Romanian engineer Dumitru had noticed the culture-based differences between hearers. "Someone hears another thing according to their culture," he told us. Culture influences hearing. What seems straightforwardly transparent in meaning to a person from one culture can be utterly misunderstood by someone from another culture. As we'll explain in this book, taking into account the specialized world of the hearer, and continually checking the hearer's understanding, is a crucial part of becoming a skilled communicator in the global office. There is no universal or worldwide hearer.

Given how speaker-centric our communication models are, it's easy to forget how key the hearer is to interpretation and understanding. It's not only Lee who assumes that the speaker is the one who has to do all the work and take all the blame; many speakers don't actually realize how much they already craft what to say or write for specific hearers (until their words are repeated to the wrong person or an email is forwarded without their consent and causes embarrassment). In the following chapters, we elaborate on this idea further. The Communication Plus model provides concrete recommendations to make the hearer the most important player in digitally mediated communication.

One thing that makes the myth of the universal hearer dangerous is the current role of English in the world. The engineers used English in their global workspaces; however, their first languages and cultures influenced how they heard and interpreted English, no matter how clearly or directly it was spoken. When Bob dramatically described conflicts with teammates across the world as "horrendous lightning storms," he saw the storms as the result of "interpreting things completely differently on both sides of the water." (In this case, the water was the Atlantic Ocean.) This metaphor of an ocean-like divide reflected the engineers' variations in hearing and interpretation habits. Many people communicating in the global workplace are using a language other than their native language. Even native speakers of the same language vary a lot in how they use language and hear it. This diversity multiplies in the global office.

Those who are native speakers and hearers of a language that becomes a global language, such as English (or Arabic, or Greek), often feel a sense of ownership over the language. They feel that how they use it is the *right* way.[7] This feeling forms the basis for hand-wringing comments that language is deteriorating, that young people don't speak very well, that immigrants speak "bad" German or English or Spanish. No matter what country you live in, you'll have heard people worry that the language is deteriorating. But language is always changing. Listen to Old English; it won't even be comprehensible to you. You're not that kind of hearer anymore.

The word *ain't*, probably the most stigmatized word in the English language,[8] was actually considered good English during the seventeenth, eighteenth, and nineteenth centuries. Educated English speakers used it. Nowadays, those who hear *ain't* are judge and jury about how dumb the people are who say it. The view that one way of hearing is "better" can cause problems in a global office because it can be interpreted as the return of oppressive colonialism.

As far as global English goes (and it seems to go far these days), depending on the country, people will feel proud about their independence, and ambivalent (if not outright negative) about their years under colonial rule.[9] In many parts of the world, one of the first tasks of newly independent governments was to create schools where the local variant of the colonial language could be taught. In many places, the colonial variant of English remains desirable as a marker of national pride. In other places, the sounds of the colonizers' English, not those of the native variant, are the ones thought to be most desirable (even if the colonizers were thrown out). A lot of Americans think that the queen's English still sounds the best, in spite of over three hundred years of independence from Britain. One study of Indian graduate students' attitudes toward English showed that 68 percent preferred the sounds of British English, 23 percent preferred the sounds of Indian English, and 5 percent preferred the sounds of American English.[10]

There is great diversity in how people hear English spoken today.[11] There is Philippine English, Nigerian English, Hawaiian English, Jamaican English, Indian English, British English, American English, and Singapore English, to name a few. In fact, nonnative English speakers outnumber native English speakers.[12] The history of English is intertwined with massive migrations of people and with colonialism. English has spread farther and has been taken on as a native language more frequently than any previous global or trade language. Despite its wide reach, though, it hasn't created universal hearers—or universal speakers, for that matter.

Even a statement as seemingly clear as "Do it the company way" can receive very different interpretations from hearers. An experienced Romanian engineer, Grigore, remembered how early on in the project, the Americans told him to do certain aspects of the design "the company way." *Okay,* he thought, *we can do that.* Over time, he and his colleagues noticed to their chagrin that each American seemed to have his or her own way to describe and implement "the company way." Sometimes it was due to their own preferences; sometimes differing interpretations of "the company way" existed. It turned out that "the company way" included not only the explicit procedures in the manual for preparing drawings or reports, but a lot of implicit knowledge about how the company was set up and functioned. Choosing the right implementation of "the company way" depended on knowing whether the managers stuck to a rigid hierarchy or chain of command, or whether it was okay to go around the boss to directly ask an engineer a question. We're not criticizing these companies for their inconsistencies; we're simply pointing out that it's not unusual for this to go on.

The company way includes the company culture, which is a complex web of employees' relationships to the organization and each other, and how these relationships are perceived and labeled.[13] Notice that in a flat organization (one that has very few levels of hierarchy), it's more likely that "the company way" can be interpreted idiosyncratically and according to individual preference. In a more rigidly hierarchical organization, on the other hand, that may be unthinkable.

Unfortunately, paying attention to the hearer and escaping the myth of the universal hearer are both made difficult in the virtual office. Conference calls and email both obscure access to hearers and their worlds. For one thing, it's impossible to get much feedback or to see puzzled facial expressions or nods of agreement. One way around this is for speakers to remember to constantly have the hearer in mind, as in our Communication Plus model. Another implication of a new focus on hearers is the idea that speakers aren't the only ones with the responsibility to generate understanding and avoid misunderstanding. Hearers have to be responsible, too. As we mentioned, we asked one of the Americans working on the American–Brazilian collaboration how he knew if he was understood by his counterparts in the other country. He answered that he didn't, and because this situation was so speaker-centered, we watched it head for trouble, mistakes, and added costs.

ALL INFORMATION CARRIES THE SAME FORCE (OR DOES IT?)

Before we present the Communication Plus model, we want to further convince you why some things needed to be added to the way you communicate now. We will pick up why a new upgrade is needed to your model with another observation we made during our time among the engineers. We observed still another belief they had about communication that caused a lot of misunderstandings: that all information carries the same force. Another way to state this belief is that directness and clarity are achievable independent of the authority of the speaker. To Americans (or those who live in more egalitarian societies generally), the notion that some information can be true, informative, or valuable only because it comes from someone with power might seem unacceptable. In fact, even in America, information has value according to its source or who said it. Moreover, in most places, the value of information is controlled by treating it as a scarce good, so it loses value if it's too freely disseminated. In places like those, some information is not easy to get.

The way that only some people's information is authorized can be shown by the way gossip moves around outside official channels. Gossipers are considered to be bad sorts of communicators who spread false or otherwise harmful information. Yet this "dark information" is highly sought after by the less powerful in a group, partly because it's unauthorized, and also because you don't have to be properly validated to possess it.[14]

Americans believe it's good to share information openly; they even call their society "the information society." Wikipedia was founded on this model of the importance of information and its free dissemination. Bob, for example, showed this belief when he told us his solution to communication problems in a global office: "Overcommunicate, share information, hope it becomes addictive." With this solution, he was assuming that all information givers and receivers are equal. To him, information was a kind of healthy drug. Because it was healthy, everyone should freely partake of it. Bob was indicating that information was so inherently valuable that more was always better than less. He also assumed that members of other cultures would be inclined to mirror the behavior he modeled, regardless of their own cultural models and beliefs. This is a view of information familiar to many Americans, but not all. Others on Bob's team realized that they'd given away too much information, which led to confusion. They began to understand that the hearer's culture influenced the ideas that hearers had about information. They also saw how information could be prioritized according to its author and its significance. As a result, they changed their strategy. They added more context to the information they did send, and they indicated the source of the information and how the information fit in with other requirements.

HOW MUCH INFORMATION?

There's yet another assumption embedded in the suggestion that direct, clear messages can avoid cross-cultural misinterpretations. That assumption (and we're up to five now, if you're counting) is that *people know how much information to give and get.* As speakers, people typically take care not to treat their hearers as less knowledgeable than themselves. So speakers tend to assume that hearers know more than they do about a certain topic. (People critiquing us during the stages of our writing this book told us we hadn't supplied enough background in some cases. We had overestimated the amount of information readers might already have.) Usually people undersupply new information because they don't want to provoke or annoy the hearer by providing too much information. When hearers get too much information, they can become insulted if they draw the conclusion that the speaker thinks they're incompetent. ("Don't talk down to me"; "Don't think I'm an idiot.") In the case of people who are truly experts, such as engineers, this dynamic can be especially marked.

Many cultures share this habit of assuming that the hearer has more, rather than less, information at hand. As a result, they have strategies for avoiding offense by not appearing to claim superiority in knowledge. One strategy is to "oversuppose" what the hearer knows and "undertell" in terms of new information, until the hearer requests clarification.[15] One of the challenges of cross-cultural situations is that some hearers are reluctant to ask for clarification. Another is finding a way to "overtell" that is not offensive and doesn't create a hierarchy of perspectives in which a speaker is seen as "talking down." For their parts, hearers need to realize that *undertelling* may be frustrating to experience, but it's also a sign of respect by a speaker rather than an exclusion or dismissal. In many of the cross-cultural encounters that we witnessed, it was unlikely that common ground was shared among the participants, so a strategy of *overtelling* would have helped avoid many of the misunderstandings we witnessed. How much in common do you and I have? It will affect how much information is "enough." Too much or too little, and a short weekly phone call about how to keep the project on target won't be as effective as it needs to be. And your cultural habits and my cultural habits will affect how this situation is resolved.

WHY DON'T WE JUST HAVE RULES?

During our research, the engineers told us some of the ways they had tried to improve their cross-cultural communication. Arjun, the engineer in Kolkata, had proposed a solution to his teammates to improve cross-cultural communication. This involved using rules. He wanted a more formal set of rules about communicating that everyone could agree on. This would help, as he put it, "to avoid any further confusion." His suggestion wasn't met with much enthusiasm by the other engineers, because they saw that it would be impossible to get any work done if, as one said, "we have to have a rule for every minor thing." They may have also recognized the enormity of the task of negotiating such rules, not to mention coming up with the rules in the first place, and enforcing their use.

Rules are a way of life for engineers, who have many rules to ensure that the complex structures they build are safe and reliable. It's easy to see how a list of rules would appeal to them. The Romanian and Indian engineers we spoke with all wanted more-explicit rules from the Americans. At one point when there was a confusion in calculations, Constantin said that further confusion could be avoided if they just had more rules about how to do things. But the Americans felt that more rules would paralyze the job. "We won't be able to proceed," an American engineer said.

One day they were discussing a complicated machinery foundation that had required a soil-investigation study before they could complete the structural design for the foundation. But then they found that some calculations had been shown on the drawings in a way that the American engineers hadn't expected. They were surprised. Everyone wanted to avoid this happening again. Constantin thought a set of rules would help avoid this in the future. But he had already caused some work setbacks by requesting another rule (in that case, that all the communications to the Romanian engineers go through him first). His rule about hierarchy worked well in the open office situation of the Romanians, where everyone could hear everything anyway, but in the global workspace, because of the limited time and opportunities for overhearing (due to dispersed work locations and time zones), it didn't work. In fact, routing all emails through him resulted in expensive delays. As a result, the Americans were wary of implementing more rules.

There are a number of problems with rules. For one thing, they have a limited utility in cross-cultural situations for the simple reason that people can keep only six or seven rules in mind at the same time. Add more rules, and their ability to process information declines. This is why cross-cultural guides are ultimately not helpful tools: they contain pages and pages of rules that are difficult to remember and execute. Add the fact that engineers need their cognitive resources for complex, novel engineering problems, and it becomes clear why a rule-based approach might hurt more than help. Another problem is that even single rules aren't very memorable unless they're practiced. Try remembering, in the moment, how many times to kiss the cheek of a French acquaintance. Is it once, twice, three times, or even four?

The best way for people to master and remember cultural distinctions is through mental shortcuts and stories. Most people can recall learning a list of rules like the Ten Commandments and being given proverbial guides for behavior by their elders, but very little of what anyone does is governed by these types of rules. People are more apt to remember the moral of the story about the little boy who cried wolf or about Henny Penny's friends who wouldn't help her make bread.[16] Descriptions of behavior are more accessible to people's memory when they're presented as sequences of related actions and consequences.

An additional problem with rules is that people can have complicated relationships with them. Everyone probably knows a clever innovator who succeeds because he or she breaks rules, or a cheeky, rebellious person who can persuade others to follow their lead. In other words, the mere existence of rules doesn't guarantee they'll be followed. Additionally, if we believe that every employee can calibrate what they say and do to a very fine degree of detail based on rational, rule-based criteria, how we can expect them to cooperate with others in the messiness of groups?

This raises an additional point about rules: Though we're writing about failures of communication, people are frequently successful at working together, and those successes can't be explained by adherence to rules. Things often have to succeed despite the rules.

People's ideas about their culture amount to a model of what culture is, just as they have a model of communication. In many people's abstract model of culture, every culture is a fixed system of rules. However, they run into a problem with their model when they visit another culture and find that as soon as they learn a "rule," exceptions spring up. That's because rules don't describe culture very accurately. Everyone creatively manipulates the rules to gain autonomy or advantage. Being able to break rules without reprisal is a sign of power (and that's a common theme across cultures). In the way that everyday life operates, rules are anything but simple, and if you look more closely at them, all societies are characterized by tensions about rules. How do rules affect autonomy? How do they influence who people can be to each other and when? These human concerns also affected the communicative interactions that we studied in companies all over the world. It's easy to wish that everyone would just stop behaving so weirdly and would conform to our own "way we do things," or follow a simple set of rules.

WHY DON'T WE JUST LEAVE OUR CULTURAL BAGGAGE AT THE DOOR?

We heard another proposal for cross-cultural communication from Andreea while we were observing and doing interviews at her engineering office in Romania. The engineering office was set back from the road behind a wire fence in a group of low industrial buildings. The offices were up a flight of stairs (where we often passed engineers on a smoking break) on the second floor. The offices were large, with generous windows, and had up to seven or eight sturdy wooden desks with computers set in rows or against the walls. Andreea told us about her strategy for working in a global office. The key was to be what she called "culture neutral." She felt that communication would be improved if everyone "checked their Romanian baggage outside." This idea had worked as a handy reminder for Andreea to stay in a flexible frame of mind in a global work setting when she was talking to people in various parts of the world. But let's look at that metaphor of checked baggage more carefully. A suitcase is something that you carry in your hand, so it's easy to drop wherever you want. But all the elements of a person's culture have been with them since early infancy, habituated in so many settings and conversations that they're impossible to abandon. They're part of who we are.

People have not only established assumptions about how communication works that can make it hard to fix problems in a global office, but also ideas about what culture is that can make miscommunication hard to fix and hard to avoid.[17] What is culture? Some people think of culture as divided into "high" culture (the Taj Mahal, Renaissance art, a certain type of manners) and "low" culture (popular music, TV). We saw this idea of "culture as civilized behavior" on João's team, where they believed that cultured people spend time during coffee and meals to get to know each other before jumping in to do business. The Americans, because they ate lunch at their desks and were always in a hurry, were considered less civilized and cultured.

To an anthropologist, culture is more than "the arts," grand architecture, food, or the objects humans have invented to adorn themselves. It's a set of habits of interpretation that everyone renews and creates in each moment of being and of doing things with other people.[18] Much of it is below the level of consciousness. Most people, if pressed, would have a hard time giving even a partial picture of it. Even anthropologists have trouble doing so; one anthropologist counted 53 definitions of culture.[19] When people on the island of Pohnpei heard Elizabeth's questions about their culture and her requests for explanations, they said, "Just watch." They were wise about the difficulties of explaining culture, especially to an outsider.

Andreea's idea of leaving cultural baggage at the door of the engineering office rests on the notion that beneath the customs (or what people can see and hear), humans are basically the same. This romantic notion can be dangerous if it justifies not learning about others' perspectives and makes someone presume that too much commonality exists. Andreea's views aren't idiosyncratic to her. Many people share the view that cultures, at heart, are all the same. They might be surprised to learn that even something as natural and spontaneous as laughter is not culturally shared. What's humorous to one culture is puzzling or confusing to another. What's so funny? We don't get it even when it's patiently explained. In a subsequent chapter, we'll talk about cross-cultural humor and its potential pitfalls.

Our globally shared human genetic inheritance doesn't cause us to have common experiences as humans. The idea of a culture-free human nature that we all share is promoted sometimes in museum exhibits and books with marvelous photographs, where people from exotic places are pictured standing with their families. The photos seem to imply that families have a lot in common—a meaning that's expected to be equally clear to everyone. But people aren't very good at estimating what other people might know. In experiments, people consistently overestimate how many other people can recognize the same things they recognize (such as celebrities, landmarks, and household gadgets). They also consistently underestimate how many people would be able to identify things they themselves couldn't.[20] Just as there's no universal hearer, there's no universal viewer, either. And the engineers working with documents with many specific visual symbols can get into trouble based on their expectations of what is shared. Recall how Dave said about the Romanian design, "It's just weird. It's not wrong, it's just weird." To the Romanians, it looked just right.

Andreea's solution of leaving culture at the door assumes that people always calculate the costs and benefits of an action before deciding what to do—that is, that they're rational. But what observers of human behavior know is that people actually behave out of habit, not logic. They don't apply rules. And the available reasons for deciding or acting in a particular way exist below the level of conscious thought. Along those same lines, Andreea assumes that people are free to make choices about how to phrase their sentences, when in fact those choices are shaped even before speakers choose them.[21]

Andreea brings up the fascinating question of what is natural and what is dependent on culture. This debate, which is often phrased as a "nature versus nurture" debate, is a very old one. New scientific evidence is challenging where we thought the line is, and if it is even a useful way of thinking about biology and culture. What we do know is that culture influences us from the first moments of breathing. One fascinating question is whether the language a person speaks influences their brain and the way their neural pathways are set up. Do we think differently from people who speak other languages? This opens the question of whether the language we speak influences how we think.

DOES OUR NATIVE LANGUAGE INFLUENCE THE WAYS WE THINK?

When we're babies and learning language for the first time, we're learning a complex system of symbols and ideas that have existed for a very long time before we entered the world. Together with learning the words for "aunt" and "uncle," we're learning a set of relationships and responsibilities. Together with learning the words for "mine" and "yours," we're learning about reciprocity. Together with learning the words for "river" and "house," we're learning (in some languages) about grammatical gender or how to classify things. When people learn a language, they learn to sort bodily, visual, aural, and tactile experience according to a scheme that's never up for question. They learn that some objects belong together in a category; for example, in their language they must use one noun classifier for counting long, thin objects and another for round objects.

Most of us live in very visually or optically oriented cultures, but some cultures privilege other sensory experiences. There are some good ways to illustrate this that bring us far from the world of engineers. For instance, the Dinka people in Africa learn to use cattle in organizing their sensory experiences in the world they share. The Dinka are a group of about four and a half million people who live in Sudan as herders and farmers. Cattle provide for them a set of conceptual categories for communicating and responding to the experience of life. A Dinka's perception and description of color, light, and shade is connected to how they recognize color in cattle,[22] and they use cattle color to describe many visual experiences that have nothing to with cows. Another example is how the Andaman Islanders (off the coast of India) use smell as the primary means to organize time, in the case of their cyclical calendar. To them, smell is the principle of life. Spirits are constantly trying to absorb the odors of the living so they can be reborn as humans. The equivalent of "How are you?" is "When/why/where is the nose to be?"[23] In the Trobriand Islands northeast of Australia, categories of smells are integral to magic, since magic must enter through the nose.[24]

People see, touch, smell, hear, and think in a tremendous variety of cultural ways. The grammar, words, and metaphors of each language provide a pattern for talking about certain aspects of the senses and the world.

So each of our conceptions of the environment is partly shaped by the way our native language creates relationships between objects, time, space, and people. In some languages you can say things like "The key opened the door," or "This is the key that will solve the problem." But for other languages it's impossible and unthinkable for an object (like a key) to do something without a person being specified to do it.[25] This shows some ways that language influences what makes sense cross-culturally. It also reinforces the need for native speakers of English to be flexible about how people use English in global English settings.

The American linguist Edward Sapir, who taught at Yale and was an influential figure in the early days of the scientific study of culture and language, strongly believed in the influence of language on thought. To this day, there remains debate about this relationship among anthropologists and linguists.[26] Sapir saw languages as "invisible garments that drape themselves about our spirit and give a predetermined form to all its symbolic expressions." The German philosopher Johann Herder described language as a "special genius" specific to each nation (or to each community in the case of India, where there are twenty-three recognized national languages).

This special genius or cloak means that in some languages the social hierarchy between individuals has to always be explicitly stated in practically every sentence or question. In Japanese, in order to refer to someone or tell a story about them, a speaker has to choose whether the person they're speaking about is higher or lower in social status; to do this it's necessary to know the age and rank of the person. In German (and many other languages), a person can't converse with someone else without indicating as they speak whether the person to whom they're speaking is someone with whom they can be intimate in certain ways, or someone who deserves to be kept at a distance.

Language not only provides many ways of socially dividing up the world around us or populating our group with invisible beings; it also influences our ideas about physical space itself.[27] In engineering school, and even earlier in science class, people have to learn new ways of seeing space—from the black holes of the solar system to the free space between electrons and the nucleus of atoms.[28] Native English speakers for the most part speak about space in terms of their own body as the center of spatial reference, using *right* and *left* to describe spatial relationships. In other cultures, an orientation toward the sea and inland or the four cardinal points are used. Someone might talk about a spoon placed east of the fork, or about the inland pair of shoes.

Language is also used in various subtle ways to avoid blaming someone or avoid anyone's taking responsibility, such as the passive voice (as in the English sentences "The men were laid off" and "Mistakes were made"), which doesn't require an agent or responsible person. Hindi does something interesting with agency and personhood. Hindi speakers often talk in terms of an inclusive self. Members of the family, friends, God, and objects and voices of parents are all included when a person describes a self that acts and is responsible in the world. The way a language habitually represents actions in a sentence has an impact on how people evaluate informal stories or complaints.

Another way that a person's native languages can influence their thought at a very deep level is through metaphors people use to understand or convey abstract or complex processes or concepts, like the metaphors of information transmission we talked about earlier. A metaphor works by taking something from one domain and applying it to another to create new meanings and associations. For instance, in Western industrialized cultures, it's familiar to think of the brain metaphorically as a sort of machine or computer. You can see this when someone says, "My brain is fried," or notes that a person with an odd personality is "wired a bit differently."

Sometimes these culturally unique metaphorical expressions are embedded in idioms and jokes; sometimes they show up in what people say spontaneously. We observed the engineers using metaphorical speech to convey to other engineers both micro and macro aspects of the work at hand. They designated some small things as very important details by using the phrase *nitty-gritty*, and they talked about how they thought about their work as a flow—and that certain actions had big consequences, like when Bob said, "If you turned off the faucet [stopped the flow of work or product] today, it would have consequences downstream [later]." They used metaphors to express emotion, to talk about engineering learning and skill building, and to talk about relationships. Meetings were a way to "nail down [decide on] timing." While discussing scheduling or pace, they talked about how they would "hit the ground running [start fast]." When an engineering problem came up, an American engineer said, "It's not a knuckle buster yet." He was referring to a phrase used by mechanics to describe working on some old American cars: in order to get a tool into the engine to fix the problem, the mechanic ended up with skinned or sliced knuckles.

These expressions made sense to those speakers using them and even influenced their ways of thinking about problems. But they weren't well understood in the global office. In one phone call, Dumitru asked Dave to explain the meaning of "passing the buck." (The phrase describes the act of passing responsibility to someone else, and the expression is supposed to have originated from the game of poker when people carried around knives with handles made from a buck's horn, and passed their knife to whoever's turn it was to deal the cards. If a player didn't want to deal, he passed the responsibility by passing the knife, or the "buck," to the next player. There are other origin stories for the phrase, too.) In Brazil, when someone is metaphorically described as deep-fried, they have a problem;[29] when someone is filling pork sausages, they are talking about meaningless issues. In Romanian, if you're told to keep your eye on something "as if it's a gas tank," you'd better keep "a sharp eye out" (a similar English idiom). The phrase about the gas tank (for natural gas) has been used since the Communist period, when there were terrible shortages of cooking and heating fuel in Romania. People had to line up for hours or days to get their tanks refilled, and there was no guarantee of supply. In Bengali, referring to someone as a *sobjanta gamchawala* ("wise towels-man") is just as unflattering as the English equivalent, a "smarty pants," used for someone who thinks they know everything and gives unwanted advice. In Bengal, the reference is to a man who sells towels (and therefore one of low status) giving advice to those higher up the chain.

Both slang and idiomatic terms, like metaphors, are problems for non-native speakers. In fact, idiom usage by nonnative speakers is interestingly different from such usage by native speakers, especially in terms of choosing when to use idioms. One study found that the proportion of slang that native speakers of English used with a boss or a friend was 23 percent with the boss and 41 percent with the friend. With nonnative speakers, however, the percentage was reversed: 40 percent with the boss and 20 percent with friends.[30] This gives you some idea of how a nonnative speaker of English might lose credibility even though it's clear that they are fluent in the language. They might be thought "too familiar" to bosses and "too distant" to coworkers, and therefore not socially intelligent or not trustworthy. Add unfamiliar idioms to this, and the complexity of the other engineer "really understanding what you mean" or how you're thinking about something becomes all too real.

As we have shown you thus far, successful communication entails a lot even between native speakers of the same language. When working with people in their own culture, most of the time people can fix communication problems because they share the same understandings of what goes wrong and how to fix it. But in cross-cultural communication, the dynamics are quite different because people don't share these understandings. What seems like a normal way of proceeding to one group causes offense in another. What is a common indirect way to communicate disagreement in one group is not even picked up by another. In order to minimize the impact of miscommunication and improve the chances of good communication occurring, it's essential for everyone to learn more about how communication works and how culture affects communication.

Many books on cross-cultural communication discuss the need to build rapport with colleagues, and they provide advice about how to do this, especially over the phone, on conference calls, or in email. While "rapport" as a kind of social connection is important, it won't solve communication problems on its own, because rapport doesn't automatically produce common ground. It also doesn't automatically provide guidance on building necessary common ground. So what is rapport good for? It's good for making relationships more resilient so that when miscommunications occur, the participants can more easily repair the relationships. However, it's not useful for helping engineers think about communication in an expanded way, as our Communication Plus model does.

A MODEL BASED ON RESEARCH WITH THE ENGINEERS: COMMUNICATION PLUS

We mentioned how people's communication models do suit most of the interactions they have with others within their own culture reasonably well. We also pointed out that the engineers found that the assumptions they had—those that we've just discussed—don't give them the tools for understanding, diagnosing, and fixing cross-cultural communication misfires in the global workplace. In the chapters that follow, we describe the Communication Plus model of communication, which is aimed at providing engineers, managers, and others with a communication model that takes culture into account and can help reduce miscommunication. The model is derived from our research and is based on our observations with engineers in the four cultures in which our research took place. It is also shaped by research done by many others. In the chapters that follow, we provide details about the five principles of this model, with specifics about how people can use it. To recap the model:

1. Language is action

Once you realize that language is really about doing things in the world (reminding, criticizing, humoring, inviting, rejecting, recognizing, disagreeing), you'll be sensitive to the fact that your language actions can be misunderstood. That's because actions aren't done in the same way in all cultures. A famous example is food offers. In some cultures, an offer of food has to be repeated three times before you can even consider saying yes to it. Before that you have to say no. It's polite to "reject" an offer of food before accepting it. Even though everyone knows these can't really be rejections and that they're really a type of pre-acceptance, they still have to be done. When someone from this type of culture comes to the United States and is offered food, they pre-accept (that is, reject) the food the first time because they know that is the right thing to do. To Americans, this first rejection is taken as a final rejection, so they don't offer the food again, and the foreign visitor goes hungry. The food offer is an action, and the pre-acceptance (or rejection) is a next action. In these and myriad other ways, each time a person speaks they're performing an action, and hearers are recognizing that a speaker is doing something, and then they react and perform a "next action"[31] that they feel is appropriate. Learning to communicate by using this idea of language as action is a crucial aspect of our model.

It's also crucial to remember that mutual understanding proceeds sequentially. One person says something—that is, does an action—and another person says something, does another action based on that, and so forth. Because many aspects of communication are routine, people become very good at predicting what might be next in a sequence, what might be upcoming, or how something might play out. People continually make inferences based on what is going on now and how sequences typically unfold, in order to prepare for what might happen. And they often use this knowledge of sequential procedures in conversation to give hints or pick up clues that conflict is upcoming. A speaker might put in a hint of disagreement before actually disagreeing, because they hope the hearer will take early steps to avoid conflict. Being aware of how these predictions work is important. If you find yourself surprised when a conversation goes in an unexpected direction, or when you find yourself suddenly in conflict with a colleague from another part of the world, there's been a misunderstanding about what was actually happening in the exchange. Because language is action, to repair these misunderstandings the participants have to attend to the actions that were taken, that could have been taken, and that weren't taken at all.

2. The hearer is the most important player

A lot of communication training, especially in corporate environments, is aimed at improving the speaker's behavior. However, this isn't sufficient in cross-cultural work settings, where the cross-cultural *hearer* is a more crucial player. If you're a speaker in these settings, you have to be vigilant about actively collaborating with hearers on meaning and comprehension. Speakers can do this by focusing more on the hearer. In the global office, everyone has to become a responsive "hearer." (We prefer *hearer* over *listener* because listening often seems like a fixed, passive role, whereas hearing seems—to us, anyway—more accurately folded into doing.) Organizations can develop ways to ensure that hearers' habits are changed as well as those of speakers. What seems paramount to us is that in the global office context, getting feedback from hearers and training them is crucial.

Research has shown that a hearer who actively communicates feedback increases their own understanding.[32] Asking what another person can see on the screen or document in front of them—especially in cases of potential cultural blindness—is surprisingly effective, even though these checks might seem small. When moving from a conventional office setting to a global work-sharing context, the hearer requires explicit attention.

3. Communication needs common ground

Communication succeeds because the participants share what is called *common ground*—a similar understanding of the topic and function of the interaction. More than simply rapport, common ground is about culture, information, and emotions. It's the past, present, and future that's made with language. In order for global teams (and any teams, really) to communicate well, they have to actively build and maintain common ground. This is harder in the digital office than when we're face to face. You might have to say what might be thought obvious. You might have to be redundant. You will have to be careful not to "oversuppose and undertell." You may have to explicitly ask people if they understand. All of this seems like a lot to remember, but in these cross-cultural interactions, in essence you're bringing your own common-ground assumptions to the other participants' attention. That's what makes this work doable—as well as exciting and interesting.

When the engineers visited each other's countries, they established common ground, but such visits weren't usually economically feasible. The alternative—using technologies such as video conferencing and conference calling—is only a partial solution. Computer-mediated interactions endanger common ground even for native speakers of the same language in the same country. They pose even bigger risks for cross-cultural communication. For these reasons, understanding the importance of common ground and how it's built and maintained is central to the Communication Plus model.

4. Language is social (and cultural)

Each language provides its speakers with the resources for building and destroying relationships. But all cultures use these resources in unique ways. When people communicate with colleagues in a global office environment, they have to focus on language in its social and cultural aspects.

This puts them in a better position to understand how what seems like a lapse or deliberate disrespect is frequently caused by someone doing what they think is right. Being indirect in telling others what we want from them, for example, might be a good strategy for preserving good relationships, but it will be harder for cross-cultural hearers to figure out. On the other hand, a strategy of being "direct" can be counterproductive: it blocks a resource that people are given by their culture to build and maintain relationships. You don't want the way you use language to undermine others' native sense of what language is for.

5. Understand that technology can be a handicap, and learn how to compensate for it

It's true that we're used to lauding technology, but it also reduces the signals and cues people depend on in communication exchanges. A lot of cues are missing from the usual face-to-face communication when we're interacting through the types of advanced technologies that make global teams possible.

In the past, a lot of informal learning about others took place through casual means, even hallway conversations, and through observing what others were doing and how.[33] Engineers (and others) now need to learn from those situated half a world away who are only partially visible, if visible at all, and only partially accessible. The engineers we spoke with were very nostalgic about face-to-face interactions with colleagues. Yet this nostalgia shouldn't get in the way of observing others and adapting one's communication for technologically mediated communication. Good strategies include increased redundancy and increased checking of understanding; but these are aspects of communication that usually aren't valued very much, so they can irritate others.

In the rest of the book, we discuss these aspects of the Communication Plus model, paying explicit attention to the ways in which the parts of this model can be incorporated into the workplace. A sociologist once defined communication as a means for fixing the problems caused by communication. This indicates that people are continually making mistakes and learning, trying to use their resources to get things back on track. We hope

Though far from the forests, lakes, and beer halls of Olde England, the engineers used what linguists and language philosophers describe as *speech acts*.[2] We want you to notice how communicating is filled with action. Once you see language as action, you'll have a key tool for solving communication problems in the global office. You'll understand that though Dave thinks that by his action he is giving a polite directive, Dumitru hears instead a by-the-way expression of what Dave prefers. In other words, Dumitru sees Dave's action differently than Dave does. Because of this gap, Dumitru is bound to disappoint Dave and slow the project down while they both figure out and correct the misunderstanding. Misunderstanding one action in a sequence can have big consequences, because it can affect subsequent actions.

But before moving to the engineering office, let's take another example from literature to reinforce how language is action. Here's a sequence from Shakespeare's *Romeo and Juliet*. Two servants of the house of Capulet, Sampson and Gregory, who hate the rival Montagues, provoke Abraham and some other Montague men at the beginning of the play. Sampson insults Abraham, a servant of the Montague family, by "biting his thumb" at him. This gesture is a powerful enough act to cause an equally powerful reaction, and a tragic tale is the result.

GREGORY. I will frown as I pass by, and let them take it as they list.

SAMPSON. Nay, as they dare. I will bite my thumb at them, which is disgrace to them if they bear it.

ABRAHAM. Do you bite your thumb at us, sir?

SAMPSON. I do bite my thumb, sir.

ABRAHAM. Do you bite your thumb at us, sir?

SAMPSON. [*Aside to Gregory*] Is the law of our side if I say ay?

GREGORY. [*Aside to Sampson*] No.

SAMPSON. No, sir, I do not bite my thumb at you, sir, but I bite my thumb, sir.

GREGORY. Do you quarrel, sir?

ABRAHAM. Quarrel, sir? No, sir.

Romeo and Juliet, 1.1.40–54

In the thumb-biting scene, there's some discussion about whether Sampson's thumb biting is intended as an insult to provoke a quarrel or reaction. Abraham is uncertain about the message that Sampson is send-ing, so he asks whether the action communicates an insult. For our pur-poses, it's a good example. In the global office, there's nothing as strange as thumb biting, but there are confusions about what action someone is doing at any one time and thus what the appropriate next action might be. These confusions caused mistakes, delays, expense, and, unfortunately, quarrels. Just as Shakespeare's character Sampson did, people often create inten-tional ambiguities. Why do they do this? To avoid conflict. Ambiguities can usually be sorted out by those who share the same cultural context, but in the global office, ambiguities (designed with a good purpose—to avoid con-flict) can actually cause conflict! In this chapter's opening scene from the forest in Olde England, insults were the game, but in the office, people are taking care to mitigate the aggressive force of language-as-action.

How do people determine what another person is doing by saying this or that, in just those words, in just this way, at just this moment? We don't usually say, "I hereby complain" or "I hereby insult you." So we have to fig-ure the action out. Language actions follow cultural patterns that people learn over time. Cross-culturally, people have difficulty recognizing them, but they can learn. How do people recognize actions cross-culturally? Partly by context, and partly by clarifying meaning with others if they feel offended or unsure. (Admittedly, the latter is not easy to do if flinging an equally offending riposte seems like the feel-good next action, rather than getting back on friendly terms.)

SPEECH ACTS

Many kinds of actions are possible in language, in addition to lobbing insults and boasts. We've used those to make a point about the power of words, but, leaving slanders and slurs aside, diverse sorts of speech acts occur in the office. There is, of course, complaining (*whinging*, or *whinge-ing*, in Indian and British English). There's also requesting, affirming, disagreeing, reminding, and promising. There's criticizing and praising. There's apologizing and thanking. There's blaming (to some people there's way too much of it) and denying, and there's complimenting (which is awkward to do well).

Everyday life is full of speech acts. Some of these you won't likely see much of at the office, though, such as praying, blessing, or betting. Speech acts like guaranteeing, pledging, predicting, intimidating, and warning occur more rarely in the office as well. Many types of speech acts surround us: accusing a driver who pulls out suddenly in front of us, asserting our place in a queue at the breakfast taco stand, objecting to having to wait once again for software upgrades to load, conjectures about a sports team's chances. There's urging the kids to get ready for school, naming a pet, offering assistance to an elderly person, directing attention to where it hurts. People give unwanted suggestions, sought-after permission, difficult commands, confident statements, incomplete descriptions, indignant assertions, pure speculations, warm greetings. We can claim and then disclaim, state and then deny, assure people, argue with them, inform others, insist we get our way, tell a good story, make a polite offer, explain why we're late, announce a discovery, acknowledge teammates, assess the kind of day it was, doubt it will get better, demand an explanation why, invite ideas for having a better day, accept some, decline others, refuse to be silenced, make a joke about it, notice it's time to drop the subject, ignore attempts to get us to move on, . . . You get the idea.

Take something like the question, Do I hear a noise? Depending on the context and people present, this question could be doing several actions, all of them plausible, but quite different from each other. It might be a directive to be quiet, as in the case of a teacher scolding a student during an exam. It could be a request for information or verification of what's happening (do other people hear a sound, too?). It could be a joke about someone's embarrassing bodily functions. How do people know what "Do I hear a noise?" is intended to provoke as a next action? Quiet? Some sort of verbal answer? Just a nervous laugh? It's both through the context (is it a classroom or an engineering office?) and observing how others are reacting.

THE POWER OF SPEECH ACTS

The power of language to do an action that changes the world and affects what happens next is great enough to be dangerous. Because people recognize this, they diminish the danger of appearing too power crazed by changing the outward appearance and force of speech acts. This involves using disguise, making one action look like some other action—cloaking a command, for example, in a request format or a question format. A teacher with noisy students during an exam could say, "I hereby order you to be quiet!" instead of "Do I hear a noise?" or "Could we please have quiet?" The first version would be crystal clear to the students. But it sounds odd for an engineer to say, "I hereby order you to send the drawings to me" or "I hereby swear an oath that I will get that mechanical specification to you tomorrow" or "I hereby inform you that from now on we will use month names and not numbers" and so on. All these sound a bit theatrical.

If people feel entitled to blatantly use their power, they can be direct in their speech acts: "Shut the door!" or "I hereby order you to close the door." But if showing power and diminishing others by forcing them to react from a weaker position isn't a good idea (which is the more usual case), a person might say, "Would you mind closing the door?" or "Did you forget to shut the door?" or "Can you think of any reason we should keep the door open?" or "I'm having trouble hearing you because of all the noise in the hall" or "Do you feel a draft?"[3] All these renderings are basically the same speech act (that is, they all direct a door to be closed), but each wears a different disguise—that of a request, an invitation for an opinion, a statement of preference, or an informational question. These disguises have the effect of appearing to give the hearer a choice to comply or to collaborate on what should be done, and they all get the job done via different paths. Yet all this becomes thorny in cross-cultural situations. One reason is that the disguises work too well for members of other cultures. They, too, disguise their speech acts, but they do so with different masks, so hearers miss the real action underneath the disguise. The hearer can seem incompetent because they don't know the English disguise and because of automatic interference from their native culture. Cloaking an action to get someone to change an engineering drawing can take many different forms across cultures. The action is the same, with the same intention to mitigate threats to another person's self-esteem or autonomy, but each culture has its own strategy for achieving this. Sometimes it can really be hard to interpret which action is the right one to do next, or what someone wants you to do next!

It's ironic that, linguistically speaking, given the millions of years of evolution that have given us the power of syntax, speech production, and perception, we mute the force of what we mean. Dave mutes the force of his action to correct a design (and mutes the action to change how something has been done) by saying, "I wouldn't do it that way" to Dumitru. (Lots of people do this, but we saw it among the engineers.) "I wouldn't do it that way" sounds like a by-the-way comment about Dave's own particular preference for doing it. It brings to mind the well-known differences among engineers in design. But he's not merely expressing his own preferences. He's actually warning or directing Dumitru to change the way he's done it. These kinds of indirect actions take place everywhere, but sorting them out in the global office seems most fraught. What's the next action for Dumitru? To register Dave and his differences as "interesting," or to change his drawing? If he doesn't understand the disguised directive, Dave will once again complain that the Romanians don't get what to do. And Dumitru will once again complain that the Americans are always changing the rules.

Indirectness in speech acts makes cross-cultural communication in an office with people from different cultures tough to interpret at times. People in most societies avoid being direct in their actions (unlike the Anglo-Saxon warriors of old), even with people they know well. Take a couple at a party. When the husband comes up to his wife and says, "Do you want to go?" you might hear her answer, "Aren't you enjoying yourself, dear?" which is a bit mystifying as a response. But she is interpreting her husband's speech act as an indirect request to leave the party. Because people tend to recycle the same indirect phrases in the same situations, the "indirect" ways become so standardized that native English speakers forget how weird they are.

Here's another example of something whose weirdness has become conventional. When people say, "Can I ask you a question?" they have already done the action of questioning. That makes it a weird thing to ask permission about. What they're really doing is using a standard disguise for interrupting you. They see you're focused on something else; they want you to focus on them, but they want to cloak their power. Another example of a strange-sounding speech act occurs when Jim says to Mike, "I promise that you will not succeed in Brazil if . . ." Is his real action that of making a promise? No, he's actually importing the gravitas of a promise action to emphasize his certainty of the outcome that Mike faces. You can start to see how things can go wrong cross-culturally when these actions or statements about the future are taken at face value, or are so weird they make no sense as directives, requests, or statements about the future. The problem is in recognizing the disguise. Only by recognizing the disguise will you be able to do the right thing next. A key to better communication is to be sensitive to action, not information. As one linguistic anthropologist said: "Language doesn't deliver meaning, it delivers action."[4]

The Communication Plus model focuses on the actions people do with their words—and how one action sets up another action as the expected next thing to do. Once you can recognize how key actions like directing, criticizing, and refusing (especially those actions that are potentially offensive) are disguised in your own native culture's way of doing speech acts, you will be better able to recognize how you yourself are disguising these sensitive but important actions. And you'll be better able to see action at work in language. Your disguises are making it impossible for your counterpart across the world to figure out what you want them to do. We can't emphasize enough the importance of finding ways to communicate to others what your speech act is and what you expect the other person to do. Hints aren't enough—yet actions still have to be done respectfully. Delivering sensitive speech acts like criticizing and directing can be done in ways that mitigate their force but don't camouflage them so heavily. This means continuing to recognize someone's autonomy when you are asking them to do something for you, but recognizing someone's autonomy through types of politeness that are more transparent, and that don't hide your real message.

In some places—like the island of Pohnpei, as Elizabeth can attest—speakers respect a hearer not through disguising actions, but through ambiguity. In other words, the more respect for the other person that a speaker adds to a speech act, the less specified content the message actually has. In Hindi and in other languages, like Romanian, using a plural pronoun (as in the Texans' *y'all*) for just one person is a way to be polite, but since it's less specific (by referring to multiple people) it could be a bit unclear. Rather than being a liability, this ambiguity is an asset. That's because it diffuses any potentially threatening force. The higher-status hearer is put in the position of deciding what next action they are being asked to do. If you think about it, this is where real power lies: the ability to determine the next action in a sequence. In a way, your average worker in a technologically connected global workplace also has that power to change the world and influence what happens next, and has culturally approved ways to mitigate the force of it.

To emphasize our points, we give examples of some ways that the engineers we worked with disguised speech acts but didn't realize they'd done so. All were ways of giving directions to other engineers. And each disguise seemed so routine that the speakers expected the camouflage to be obvious—and therefore thought the message they softened would be obvious. You'll notice in these examples that the native English speakers often use *let's*, as in "Let's make sure this calculation is done correctly," even if they're commanding a specific "you," as in, "You better make sure this calculation is done correctly." Sometimes *we* is combined with a "need" statement rather than a directive, as in "We need to make sure there is enough room to maintain that valve." They may really mean that the other person should make sure to change the design. In some of the meetings and phone calls we observed, an engineer said "we" but meant "you" instead. "We" sounds more collaborative and less directive, but the result is an impenetrable disguise.

WAYS THE ENGINEERS CAMOUFLAGED ACTION WITH LANGUAGE (MOSTLY NATIVE ENGLISH EXAMPLES)

Framing an order as an act of kindness expected from someone

- *"Do me a favor. Just run across this for a second."* Here, "Do me a favor" makes something look like a request for an act of kindness but is really an order the speaker expects not to be refused. "Do me a favor" is often used by native English speakers when they are asking someone to do something that involves extra work or is a little annoying for that person.

Framing a "you do it" as "we'll do it"

- An engineer in Houston says: *"Let's go back and get that bypass line."* Here, "let's" looks like a "we" action, but the action is really expected to be done by only the engineer in Romania.

- Cynthia says, *"Let's make it one inch because otherwise . . . "* She's framing as a "we" action an action that's really expected to be done by Andreea across the world in Romania.

- Dave says to the American engineer Larry during a conference call with India: *"Well, let's not focus too much on these, Larry."* Dave frames his directive to Larry to move on to the next item on the agenda as a "we" action, but it's only Larry's behavior that's supposed to change. Dave's agenda is made more important. Dave also uses the mitigating phrase "too much," which is a gentle way to say the level of Larry's focus was in question, not what he was focusing on.

Asking what looks like an informational question but is really a directive

- During a model-review conference call between the United States and Romania, Pete says: *"What are those blue boxes doing there below the nozzles? That's going to be snug."* He's using an information question to criticize and to decertify the way something was done by the Romanian team. "That's going to be snug" describes a vague outcome, using an uncommon English word (*snug*) that the Romanians are supposed to realize is a negative characterization.

- *"Is that pipe right along the ground? Will we have to be stepping over it all the time?"* This is an informational question that criticizes something in a drawing, asking another professional to agree with a negative assessment of their own solution.

- *"Do we really need a double block?"* This is criticism framed as an informational question.

- *"Can we make that water line at the top more accessible?"* This appears to be a question about ability. What's really meant is "Change that," and in a particular way.

- *"I'm curious, for lack of a better word, what is going on with that middle purple line."* This is a shocked reaction to a design and means, "You'd better rethink it."

Expressing a directive as merely a personal preference

- *"I don't like the configuration."* The disguise is personal preference, but it means that something must change.

Framing an order as conditional ("if")

- *"If you could put that valve by the platform . . ."* The disguise is tentativeness, but the statement is really a directive.

Using a need statement

- *"Okay, see here, see this drain? That's not really needed, guys."* The disguise is to reject a person's idea based on needs. Then it's further mitigated through the friendly use of *guys*.

Withholding a negative reply or refusal action

- The Indian and Brazilian engineers often thought not giving an answer would be interpreted by Dave and Joe as a disguised *no* to a request. However, the Americans interpreted the silence as a disguised *yes*.

Withholding bad news:

- The Indian team didn't communicate that they weren't able to meet the schedule. They did this to avoid the action of raising a conflict (and ended up too optimistic about being able to catch up if things got behind).

Using English as if it were a different language

When the Romanians used English as if it were Romanian, the results were often very "bald" directives, because English lacks the feature of Romanian grammar that allows for the insertion of politeness on pronouns. In Romania, there's the choice between the casual *you*, the respectful *you*, and the honorific *you*. Each pronoun has its own way of disguising a directive or request, or mitigating its force.

The example below illustrates the difficulties of recognizing disguised actions over the course of an interaction. The surface form of person A's "I wonder . . ." is not seen as a directive to *change* the piping design, but as a request for more *information* about it.

Table 1   Underlying actions during an interaction

Person in an action sequence	Surface form (what it seems to say)	Underlying action
Person A	"I wonder about this choice."	Indirect command ("Change this!")
Person B	"Let me assist your thinking process"; gives information.	Responds with information to "wondering" statement since Person A seems curious; happy to go on and on about their design idea and glad it's received well
Person A	"It'll have to be changed."	Annoyed that their indirect command to change it has to be repeated; feels entitled to be more aggressive
Person B	"Well, okay, but we've done it this way on other jobs."	Feels treated rudely, not valued

First Action: Person A (native speaker): "I wonder about your choice to put that pipe there."

Surface meaning: "I'm thinking about your choice."

Effective translation of disguise: "You'll have to move it to a place that makes more sense (and doesn't make me have to think why)."

Second Action: Person B (nonnative speaker): "Well, here's my thinking: I put it there because . . ."

Surface meaning: Gives more information, offers help.

Next Action: Person A: "Look, it's just not done that way to have the water line there."

(Person A is annoyed to have to repeat himself, because there's so much that still needs to be done.)

Next Action: Person B (becoming defensive): "Well, we've done that on other projects. . ."

Both B and A feel that the other's actions are confusing and reveal an uncooperative spirit. And yet both were trying to be collaborative and cooperative. We'll be focused here on the way that people try to manage the risks of telling other people what to do and manage the risks of acting in a way that might be seen as aggressive or selfish, and not collaborative.

INITIATING AND RESPONDING ACTIONS

We'll soon return to the steel high-rises of engineering firms, but keep in mind the idea of the power of language to insult and its action function.

Missing a first action and doing the wrong "next action" can lead to an expensive chain of mistakes, and to damaged relationships. The next action could be thought of as the next action in a familiar script. Across cultures, some speech acts automatically trigger scripts, like the examples from Olde England. Remember how João complained that the Americans got right down to business and didn't show personal regard for him? This had to do with greeting sequences or scripts. One important initiating action or speech act that everyone has in their culture is a greeting. A greeting is an action plus a next action sequence (and so on, until the greeting has been done right). Greeting actions are supposed to build on each other. This means there are variations in how many actions and responding actions it takes to accomplish a greeting without seeming rude or uncaring. Americans in some cases sent emails without a greeting. In other cases, the greeting was minimal. João didn't say that Joe didn't greet him, but that when he did, it was worse than nothing. The action wasn't wholly absent, but it seemed to João insincere. That's because Joe's greeting sequence was abbreviated. He didn't leave very many spaces for João's responses. Leaving out so-called pleasantries ("How is your family?"; "What's the weather like there?") might be intended as a way to avoid delays, but pleasantries are also actions that build trust, and show respect and interest. Romanians who travel to the United States are shocked at the greeting sequences of Americans. Although Americans ask "How are you?" as part of their greeting sequence, Romanians notice that no one really wants to hear their answer. The greeting sequence in the United States is often so short that the "How are you" action is not expected to be answered with anything but "Fine!" And the conversation moves on to other actions.

Extended greeting sequences, though, are important actions that build common ground and valuable contextual information—the kind of contextual information people need to work together successfully in a team. Context is especially vulnerable to being lost in email and other forms of electronic communication. It's true that extended greeting sequences are difficult in conference calls because it's hard to know who's responding to a greeting on a group conference call. It may seem easier to get to the agenda rather than navigate many voices speaking at once. But greetings provide emotional information and other information to build on, and allow people to better design the "right" responses in the future. So if people leave out the actions of exchanging "pleasantries" during greeting-action sequences, they're probably wasting time in the long run, because they're damaging social ties they'll need later.

People use their knowledge of sequences of initiating and responding actions to predict what might happen next and to figure out what's expected of them or what to do next. A question, for example, calls for an answer as the next action to do. If you don't answer, people will pursue you until they get an answer! A person who asks a question starts an action sequence (the same as in greetings) that's going to be played out (in different ways in different cultures, as scene 3 of the introduction showed). A question can be a great way to start a new action sequence because it works so well to get people's attention. One day, during an especially frustrating conflict about a design feature, Don suddenly asked a question that stopped the sequence of arguing. He initiated a change in the projected sequence of actions (a long, tiring back-and-forth disagreement). He did this by asking, "Can I say something?" (one of those weird questions, given that he just did say something!). When Don had everyone's attention, he gave a directive in the form of a question about ability. "Can somebody draw a sketch and send it to us before we start changing everything?" he asked. "So can somebody spend five or ten minutes and do a sketch?" In fact, everyone stopped arguing and agreed they could, and the sketch became the focus of everyone's attention.

Understanding the relationship between initiating and responding actions can help make sense of what happens next and also what went wrong when someone replies in an unexpected way. Then repairs can be made by going back to the initiating action.

MAKING PREDICTIONS

When they are about to do an action, such as a request, people often try to check out the temperature of the water, so to speak, before jumping in with their request. That is, they try to get a sense of how a request might be received, favorably or unfavorably (what the responding action will most likely be), before making the request. And as they are checking out the water, their very act of checking the water is used by the hearer to make predictions so *they* can be ready for the upcoming action they'll have to respond to. Here's an example. Say Dave calls up Arjun and asks (after the greeting sequence), "Hey, Arjun, have you all got a lot of work right now?" Arjun can answer something like "Not compared to last week," or "Not really," or "Yes, we're really busy." So Dave has found something out about the likelihood of his request for Arjun's team to do some work being granted, and Arjun has been alerted that a request is upcoming. If Arjun predicts that Dave's question about how busy they are is a precursor to making a request, he might think before answering about their workload and say something like, "We're not that busy today, but tomorrow we've got a big job coming in." Dave will then use this information to decide whether to make his request. Dave might not make his request for help at all but look to another source instead. This avoids Dave's getting a rejection and Arjun's losing face by having to deny the request. It turns out English speakers often design actions such as requests with "pre-requests" to test the water. You can see once again how cultural information comes into play to interpret a language action and how people use one action to know what might be coming next.

Avoiding rejection is something that goes on all the time. People design their questions and requests in ways that avoid rejection. They even design them to hint to someone else what answer they prefer to get in order to maximize the likelihood of acceptance and minimize the likelihood of rejection.[5] In a study of ten languages, confirming answers were sometimes six times more frequent than disconfirming answers.[6] This shows a cross-cultural preference for avoiding rejection and preferring agreement. This is something to keep in mind when things get tense in the global office: nobody wants it.

Designing a question in a negative questioning form that begins "Don't you . . ." indicates that the next action you want a person to do is to agree with you. It also puts pressure on the responder.[7] When Dave says, "Wouldn't you rather put a larger valve there?" he's trying to get João to realize that he prefers a positive response or agreement. People who work together make sure that their actions work and design their requests to get agreement, so they don't get their proposals or needs rejected by others.

People also prefer not to reject requests of others. A signal that a request is about to be denied is often given to soften the blow. This gives the requester a chance to withdraw the request and avoid rejection altogether. Let's say we make a request to someone who then hesitates before answering us, and we predict that our request is likely to be turned down. We might then jump in with a slightly modified request that *could* be granted. When people sense hesitation after they've made a request, they often reformulate the request to offer a chance to provide an agreeable answer. In other words, they try to preempt the person's rejection. No one likes to get rejected. There is a great example from a book on linguistic anthropology:[8] A student says to a teacher, "So I was wondering, would you be in your office on Monday, by any chance." There is then a two-second silence—a notable delay in answering a question, by American conversational standards. After this long delay, the student then says, "Probably not."

Notice that it's the student who's speaking the whole time. We don't even hear anything from the teacher. Why does the student answer his own question and answer it with a negative? Precisely because the teacher hasn't answered—but instead has maintained a two-second silence. The student knows that rejections are typically delayed, so he has predicted that the teacher's answer is no. The student then makes it possible for the teacher to agree and not reject the student's request (and say something such as, "You're right, I'm not going to be in my office"), so that instead of rejection, agreement is the next action. There's a Brazilian joke that illustrates how people regularly predict what's upcoming. The joke goes like this: A daughter goes to her father and asks him, "Hey, Dad, can you give me fifty bucks?" The father replies, "Forty dollars? What do you want thirty dollars for? Twenty-five dollars is a lot of money, dear. I can give you ten." The dad leapfrogs the whole predictable bargaining sequence.

Avoiding rejection by predicting what's coming next can reduce the overt appearance of power moves. Let's talk about power relations for a moment.

POWER RELATIONS AND ACTIONS

As Arjun told us, he found the Americans sometimes too painfully direct, but he realized that directness made things more understandable. If we follow Arjun in advocating being more direct in order to prevent the misunderstandings that are caused by using disguises in directives and requests, we need to talk about power relations and hierarchy at the office. Being direct can seem rude because it assumes one person has the right to order someone else around or that one person's needs are paramount. Since overt displays of power are risky and inadvisable in work teams, something has to be done to soften the blow. Roger said at one point: "We have to tell Romania why we are making the change, not just say, 'Do this.'" He was responding to complaints by Dumitru and Constantin about their team feeling put down.

Directives and requests set up power asymmetries that can be offensive. Let's consider requests first. Requests concern us here because they're a big part of office work and make up the highest proportion of emails. Requests influence someone else's future actions. And they can be an imposition. Most people cringe when someone asks to borrow something they themselves consider essential. Despite the frequency with which people in professional contexts use them, requests are delicate and easily set the scene for hierarchy to come into play, leading to personal affront and irritation.

People know that power management during requests is important. Even if there's a strong formal hierarchy in place, you'll find that even powerful bosses lessen the force of their requests (unless they are using directness to display their anger or it's an emergency).

Power problems with requests in a face-to-face office setting (not the global office) are usually reduced through a history of give-and-take between individual engineers. Engineers who work together in the same office building develop a history of give-and-take for help. Over time, this pattern leads to a sense of whether a person feels entitled to request help.[9] You might say that an informal set of permissions develops. These informal permissions influence whom an engineer is most likely to request help from, or whom a person can feel comfortable interrupting or asking for an opinion from. In the global office, it's hard to duplicate this history of give-and-take, which isn't written down or formalized and is therefore difficult to rely on.

How did the engineers deal with the power of request actions in their global setting? The engineers had strategies for avoiding irritating other engineers when they had to impose on them, and for not appearing to claim superiority, but sometimes these didn't work as well in a global office as they did at home. In many languages, using very polite pronouns and certain types of word forms while making requests automatically makes the requests more palatable in ways that aren't possible in English. So in some languages you can do something like, "You of higher status than me, high-status-ly change the drawing, or high-status-ly send the drawing to me." These forms are usually lost when translated into English, since there's no equivalent.

Making requests polite (in ways that preserve relationships) in English can be very subtle; even the choice between using the words *would* and *could* in requests depends on two things: how hard the speaker thinks it will be for the other person to comply with a request and how entitled the speaker feels to ask for something. (Some people think *would* is more polite than *could*.) If Arjun picks a more "entitled" form—"Could you do it right away?"—Dave might feel put in the one-down position. As Arjun explained, "You are dealing with a foreign country, foreign code, a code that is in flux that can be challenging. We were trying not to send too many messages or too many mixed messages." But he laughed. "Actually, we should expect mixed messages."

One morning in Houston, Cynthia asked Dumitru for a delivery date for some drawings: "Can you give some dates? Can you give some approximate dates? By the end of this week do you think?"

Dumitru answered with one word: "No."

Robin then said, "Okay, what . . . what target date?"

Dumitru answered, "Uh, one week. At least one week."

Here Dumitru first answered in a very direct way. Robin then stepped in to do the next action—a more collaborative way of asking about timetables. (Cynthia had leapfrogged from a general question to a very specific one very quickly). Rather than suggesting a time, Robin returned to a version of the more open-ended question about time that Cynthia had started with—"What target date?"—increasing the possibility for Dumitru to have a say. Requests can be delicate, because the inability to fulfill someone's request can lead to a loss of face if, for example, someone believes they will be seen as a person who is not reliable or effective.

Because it's dangerous cross-culturally to rely on hints and disguises to get things done, we advocate designing directives and requests with a particular hearer in mind and not just relying on habits of disguise for requests and directives. Remember that many languages solve the problem of the hierarchy that requests and directives bring out by choosing a polite pronoun or polite verb (and in that way directly showering respect on the person). This is the case for three of the four native languages of the engineers in this book. However, English doesn't have polite pronouns anymore. (A few centuries ago, a person could switch between *thou* [singular] and *you* [plural] to show respect, but over time the polite form [*you*] became more and more common, eventually displacing the more familiar *thou* altogether, leaving English speakers without a way to show respect via pronouns to lessen the force of their directives and requests.) Politeness, though, can still be added by using other common forms, such as the phrase "with all due respect," and in many other ways.

Should everyone speaking global English be more direct? Directness is no panacea. It also comes with its own risks. One summer afternoon in Romania, as we were sitting in on a conference call with American and Romanian engineers, Mike in the United States interrupted Dumitru, who was defending a Romanian proposal for an engineering modification. Mike said to him: "Okay, no. Anybody at any moment at any time gives you instructions, you have to do them." Dumitru replied: "Okay, Mike, okay we start to be crazy." So when directives and requests are made *too* baldly (as had been done by Mike), they can be seen as irrational, and the requester as irrational. The key is to be aware of your own common disguises and to adapt to giving and hearing more direct requests—ones that are both polite and that leave an opening for give-and-take collaboration.

Looking at language as action means being alert to ways that people initiate and respond to action sequences. When a person is initiating an action, they are often concerned with staying clear of asserting power. This means people can't expect their colleagues across the world to just be direct or just "say what you mean!" However, once people get used to analyzing what action they're trying to do, they can try to make the action polite without disguising it and without making it impossible to interpret. In the thumb-biting scene of *Romeo and Juliet*, there's some discussion about whether thumb biting is intended as an insult to provoke a quarrel or reaction. And even Sampson clarifies with Gregory, "Is the law of our side if I say ay?"

As Sampson and Gregory (in the Shakespeare play) knew, whatever language action is done by one person sets up a corresponding action, and whatever is said next will be interpreted as part of the action chain. If someone says something that you didn't expect next, this is clear feedback that something about your action wasn't understood.[10]

In addition to requests and directives, criticism as an initiating action can seem as threatening as yelling insults across a medieval lake, so it's sometimes disguised. Constantin said, "One day they email and say I'm doing a great job, but then the emails seem to say, 'You guys don't know what you're doing.'"[11] This indicates that the disguises may have been too effective.

Both a person's initiating and responding words act in ways that people are familiar with when they're on their own cultural ground, but can act in ways they don't intend when they're communicating in cross-cultural situations. This means people can still be in trouble even if they don't use any of the four thousand types of insults Shakespeare's characters used, like "Thou infectious unchinsnouted barnacle."[12] Sometimes people get lucky and a different intentionality is taken into account when they unintentionally offend. Other times people take offence even if they know that the behavior wasn't intentional.[13] People who aren't in *flyting* contests dislike rude, aggressive actions. All the engineers disliked them, too.

USING TECHNOLOGY

The ability to project ourselves into the "virtual" intercultural space of the global office involves a tremendous loss of cultural, environmental, and nonverbal context.[14] This affects the resources that people have for building common understanding. As a result, the ways people typically do language actions sometimes don't work right.[15]

The ways that people have developed to get things done have been worked out face to face over millennia, but digitally mediated conversations are relatively new on the scene. And in technologically mediated conversations, which include requests, directives, criticism, and many other speech acts, there is ample room for misunderstanding when you have only a computer screen to respond to or a phone set.[16] The technologically mediated speech act is often devoid of human touch for many reasons: there's no mitigating body language, no information about how long the person has been waiting to talk to you, and variant cultural signals for showing politeness and respect.

In the time pressure that seeps into cross-global conversations (people often have workdays that overlap only by an hour or two), you might, like Dave or Don, at times want to dash off a quick, direct email: "Just do it," or "We have to have your calculations on the reactor today." However, it's not only the reactor that's going to be reacting if there's no added acknowledgment of the stresses of affecting someone's future actions. The email's words are indisputable in their meaning, but something important is lost: people might feel unappreciated for their efforts, particularly since cross-cultural work life is already stressful, with nasty surprises sometimes. Your desk is full of things that took longer than you expected, and there's a stack of unanswered email in your inbox. Making a request of someone is an action—not as dramatic an action as in *flyting* perhaps, but deserving of a proper flourish that gives recognition and respect to your hearer, the person whose attention and goodwill you need for the show to go on. They are probably short on recognition and time, just like you. What we're suggesting here is that speech acts be made up of action plus respect, but that the respect not be in the form of a disguised action—rather, that the respect be in the form of another kind of acknowledgment of the other person.

With technological mediation, actions can't be done in the same way as they are face to face. It's necessary to acknowledge others through means that will be heard, as the Brazilian engineers said—to take some time to do the work of developing friendly and trusted relationships—so that when the tough acts come or have to be followed, common ground has been established, and relationships are more resilient.

To recap:

- Language is action, and saying something is part of a series of actions.

- When one action is performed, such as requesting, directing, or giving feedback about something or someone, this limits the actions the other person can perform. If someone doesn't say the expected thing, it means they didn't understand your action.

- Because people get used to how others in their culture accomplish things with language, people can often guess at which actions are upcoming in exchanges with others from their culture. Cross-culturally, though, this ability to guess is diminished. You may think you gave a big hint that you were going to reject a design, but your colleague across the world really had no idea.

- People have different cultural habits for performing actions with language, so it's important to look not just for information, but also for underlying actions.

- Meaning is a process of collaborative, alternating action between speaker and hearer. How an action is "heard" or understood and what's done next depend on cultural habits.

One way to put all this into action in the global office is to expand and repeat what you want done or what you're requesting. Another is to be aware of your own culture's disguises. Yet another is to consider the hearer, which is what we take up in the next chapter (along with the hearer's role), and to develop your skills as an effective cross-cultural hearer.

3 The Hearer

You scullion! You rampallian! You fustilarian! I'll tickle
your catastrophe!

Henry IV, Part 2, 2.1.58

Let's talk about profanity. Not every culture has profane words, but quite
a few do, and they range from the sacred to the taboo, words that people
utter when they're mad or frustrated. When Dutch speakers are profane,
they even throw in a few diseases: when a person dangerously cuts them
off in the bike lane, they might wish cholera, smallpox, or the plague on
the offender. At these moments of seething raw emotion, the speaker feels
better becoming a swearer. Some odd research has even shown that people can withstand pain better if they swear and bear.[1]

But in spite of the benefits of swearing, the speakers aren't the ones
who count, nor does their pain threshold. It's hearers who are the crux of
successful interactions. The offensiveness of swearing isn't intrinsic in the
words but in the reaction of hearers. If we reflect on this, we realize the
power that hearers have over speakers. In Europe's medieval times, hearers could send speakers to jail or even order their tongue cut out.[2] They
could have them branded with a hot iron. Even now, in some countries
swearing is against the law.[3] The Dutch have their League against
Blasphemy and Swearing (*Bond tegen het vloeken*), and a U.S. government
agency censors radio and TV programs for "offensive" speech. (Comedian
George Carlin has a famous skit on the seven dirty words that can't be

used on radio or television.) This shows that hearers who have a certain power and authority can claim power over speakers who haven't said anything yet.

We're going to take this notion from the world of swearing—that hearers can influence speakers and verbal situations—and apply it to all communication more broadly. We're even going to go so far as to say that a good way to improve your communication in the cross-cultural global office is to recognize this one thing: the hearer rules. (Which doesn't mean that we're advocating swearing; read on.)

We're saying something about the hearer's important role, which isn't usually included in most descriptions of communication, from the theoretical to the everyday.[4] Neither is the hearer part of the way in which Dave, Dumitru, João, and Arjun often spoke to us about who was responsible for making communication succeed. Like Dave, Dumitru, João, and Arjun, most books about communication focus on speakers and their roles. These expert sources don't have much to say about hearers or listeners at all.[5] That doesn't help people in the global office, a place where the hearer becomes the most important player, the crux of the effectiveness of an exchange or a relationship. Hearers are important because who they are, the cultural modes by which they hear, their culture's sense of what makes a "proper" person, and all the other dimensions of language-as-culture determine the effectiveness of communication. In this context, if you don't account for the hearer, your communication is going to fail.

If most people were asked, they'd probably agree that hearers are important, but they wouldn't go so far as to say that hearers are the *most* important. Many people believe and many books propose that when something communicative goes wrong, the problem lies in what the speaker said. It wasn't in how hearers were neglected by the speaker or in how hearers weren't included. Most people's models of communication tell them that when something goes wrong, you have to backtrack to the speaker's intent to sort it out and fix it.

A very plain illustration of this was an incident between Cynthia and Dumitru. A serious and expensive delay of two full days (involving at least twenty people) on a project that was already behind had everyone complaining. It turns out that Dave had written an email, the kind he writes every day, in a way that he was used to using when writing emails about stages of the engineering project—a way he'd used hundreds of times for his Houston colleagues. But Dumitru and Andreea, in reading Dave's email in the shadow of the Carpathian Mountains, with the region's history of kings, queens, and oil fields, read it according to their own context and experience as hearers. In other words, there were *multiple* cultural hearers.

Cynthia took time from the project itself (falling further behind schedule as she did so) to reread the email, hoping to determine what had happened. She wasn't simply going to swear at her colleagues as rampallians or blockheads. And she wasn't trying to clarify what Dave really meant. Rather, this time she read Dave's email with another hearer's interpretation in mind. She knew that Dumitru and Andreea had reacted to this email not very favorably. She just had to reverse-engineer their response. When she reread that email, she told us, she realized she had "looked at the email from American eyes" only. Someone sitting near her would have heard her say, "Oh." It was a small, quiet "oh," but it represented a huge transformation in her understanding.

Cynthia realized that she could "send email all day long," but that "if they don't interpret it correctly, things get lost when you're talking across the ocean." She meant the physical ocean, but it's a cultural ocean, too.[6] And when she uses the phrase "interpret it correctly," you'll notice that she comes dangerously close to putting the focus on the speaker's intent as the crux of the issue, as her model of communication says she should. But she doesn't do this. Instead, we think she's really building the hearer's experience into the definition of *correct*. She's realizing how critical it is to treat hearers as central, to expect differences in hearing, and to get feedback from hearers about their understanding. This is an important advance in her thinking about communicating cross-culturally, as we'll show.

But this idea isn't particularly new. One of the most influential and widely quoted experts on communication, Aristotle, believed that of the three parts of communicating (as he saw them over two thousand years ago)—the speaker, the topic, and the audience—it was the audience that was most powerful in determining the success of the communication outcome. And philosophers continue to emphasize the work hearers have to do when they infer what speakers are getting at,[7] and how language principally acts to facilitate understanding between *two* people.[8] In psycholinguistics, too, the hearer's role is considered to be a very active rather than a passive process. Research more recently has shown that hearers influence even the number of words a speaker uses when referring to something.[9]

A hearer isn't simply playing a role that's set up by the speaker, as Cynthia indicated with her comment. It can be more useful to look at things in the opposite way: the speaker is playing a role that's set up by the hearer. Take an example of someone launching a campaign against smoking. The shape that the antismoking message takes is going to be largely determined by its target audience. If it's going to teenagers, it ought to take one form; if it's going to parents, it ought to take another. A similar dynamic exists along the cultural dimension. Someone who lives in an achievement-oriented culture might assume that to convince a smoker to quit, the antismoking message ought to emphasize how quitting smoking can improve a person's chances of achieving an important goal. But if the audience comes from a culture where high achievement is ridiculed as shallow and selfish (often termed a "tall poppy syndrome," because taller-than-usual poppies will be chopped down), this wouldn't be an effective way to craft a message. It would be better to appeal to the effect of smoking on *other* people. Even temporarily putting the speaker in the hearer's role has a positive effect on communication. Unlike writers of antismoking ads, the engineers don't have the luxury of being able to rethink and revise what they say; instead, they have to react in the moment. But they can benefit from engaging the hearer; communication in the moment can be revised, too, as the hearer's responses are taken into account, if the focus shifts from being exclusively on the speaker.

The engineers told us that when they traveled across the ocean, communication really improved. For example, Phil was sent from America to India for several weeks, and because communication improved subsequently, Dave attributed it to Phil's ability to "force them to provide information." We have a different interpretation, though. We think Phil's visit improved communication overall because he learned how to craft his messages for different cultural hearers. Face to face with his counterparts for the first time, he had more immediate feedback from them as hearers. In turn, that enabled him to more easily put himself in the hearers' shoes. Additionally, he could observe many Indian hearers and differences among them, which also helped.

HEARERS

Hearers are the unsung heroes of communication. We don't exaggerate when we say that all their work mostly goes unrecognized. We know that when people hear profanity, their skin conductivity changes, their blood flow fluctuates, and they begin to sweat. People who are listening are doing much more than processing sound. In fact, speech perception involves using multiple sensory modalities. You've probably experienced how you hear differently if you can watch someone's lips move rather than just hearing their voice. We tend to forget about the amount of work we hearers are doing to respond to and to make sense of speakers. In writing this book, we authors are trying to put ourselves in the role of readers, too, assuming things about you. We're assuming that you're somewhat achievement oriented and curious, enjoy cross-cultural contexts, and have very little time. We believe that how you interpret what we write is influenced by the groups you belong to and want to belong to.

To better illustrate how much work hearers do, let's take an example a bit far afield from the desks of João, Arjun, Dave, and Constantin. We're on the island of Great Britain, observing as one British person asks another, "Have you had your tea?" and the other person, the British hearer, answers, "Yes, I had sausage and chips," never mentioning the tea beverage. (In a phrase like this used in Britain, *tea* refers to the evening meal, not the beverage.) In fact, a popular, long-running U.K. sitcom called *You'll Have Had Your Tea Then?* uses the meaning of *tea* as supper, while at the same time illustrating the concept of the importance of the hearer and the work that hearers have to do to make sense of speakers. The sitcom title refers to the fact that hearers have to interpret "You'll have had your tea then?" not so much as a real question as a subtle indication that they, an unexpected suppertime visitor, won't be fed. (The sitcom isn't about rudeness, but pokes fun at Scottish thriftiness and its consequences.) Ironically, the person who's just dropped in will probably get only a cup of tea. The British hearer understands that the sentence "You'll have had your tea then?" isn't a question but an announcement of what's going to happen next: no supper for you.

Another example of the work hearers do is the signals they give. For instance, hearers can preempt offers before a speaker makes them. When hearers anticipate that an offer is going to be made and already know they'll reject it, like when someone asks, "Are you doing anything tonight?" a hearer might quickly reply with details about their busy schedule. Hearers like this are doing the work of protecting the speaker's feelings by cutting off delivery of an invitation and sparing them rejection.

So when Mike told us one morning that he realized the engineers needed to "be very careful" that all of the comments they sent across the ocean were "not ambiguous in any way," and that every comment should "stand on its own," we knew that he was dangerously ignoring the hearer's part in the collaborative effort of making sense and getting work done. Comments never stand on their own, and hearers play a crucial role in making sense of communication. The hearer is not just a partner in figuring out odd questions. Hearers also use a person's accent and speech style to predict that person's future behavior or to divine their traits, such as trustworthiness, believability, ability to help them get the job done, cooperativeness, and attitude toward authority. Hearers match the vocabulary and speed of speakers and make judgments about their competence, sociability, and credibility.[10] Even small changes in voice quality are immediately sensed by hearers and affect what they say or do next.[11]

Cultures can vary in how much of a role is given to hearers. In African-American culture, people are taught how important the hearer is.[12] In other groups, too, hearers are recognized as doing the most important work. Samoans believe that you have to get the hearer to recognize what you're doing[13] and collaborate with them. Many of the signals hearers give to speakers, though, are visual cues, like facial expressions and body stance, and these signals are often unavailable to engineers and others working in global offices. The verbal sounds that tell a speaker, "Go on, I'm following you," such as "Mmmhmm" in English, are hard to convey through an audio-only conference call with several participants. So the hearer has to be brought into the collaboration in explicit ways.

Hearers do so much active work in communication that the word *hearer* seems too passive. That's why we prefer *communication partner*, as in a tennis partner. Good communication involves anticipation and return, as in games of tennis, squash, or racquetball. Since everyone's been playing the game for years, volleys and returns come habitually, until something that's in bounds is called out. (By comparing communication to a game, we're not saying it's either fun or low stakes. We're saying participants can have many different ways of playing but still ostensibly be engaged in the same activity.[14])

One afternoon when we were talking with Don and Dave, they told us that they realized they were ignoring the hearer and the way their hearers thought about what's "fair" and "foul" in the communication game. Don said, "We just fling information out, and the Indians, instead of asking, 'What the heck are you saying?'—they'll just sit there and they'll nod and go on. Then they have to figure it out later, instead of saying, 'What are you taking about?'" Don and Dave here give a good description of the energy required of a hearer to communicate well. The problem is that they realized too late how to account for it in the moment.

Cynthia ran into the active role that the hearer plays in communicating. And Dumitru did, too. He said he didn't allow his engineers to send emails without his overview because he had found that "things can explode" if his engineers were heard in a way they hadn't anticipated and people ended up feeling angry and frustrated.

It's true that in email, as in other written texts, it's hard to experience the hearer as active. Writers have to project or guess what sense the hearer or reader is going to make of their words and, in the case of work emails, their requests, questions, and other actions. Email is surprisingly good at stimulating irritation and hurt feelings in hearers or readers. It's easy to read an absence of relationship-building actions at the beginning of the email as evidence of an unpleasant tone or personal attack. Books and articles on communication suggest that offense in emails can be caused by brevity and not enough context. However, we feel that a bigger reason is that the hearer's input in collaborating on the message is missing. The work that hearers do in face-to-face communication is forgotten or undervalued. And because people haven't realized the crucial part the hearer plays, they don't even know how to fix email problems. People put in exclamation marks and smiley faces to reach out to the hearer, but even those don't work very well. The exclamation marks can seem to add a note of hysteria, and the smiley faces may seem too tabloid.

Forgetting about the active role of hearers, or acting like the *speakers'* intent or meaning is foremost, can be rather insulting to the hearer. It can be heard as the speaker claiming a higher social status than hearers, which damages work relationships. When people think they haven't been treated right as hearers by a speaker's words, what underlies their reactions is the feeling that the power hierarchy has been misconstrued. They may also feel that a person is using power beyond what is considered legitimate.[15]

At the end of the first project kick-off meeting, Constantin complained about being an unrecognized hearer. He told us that the Americans had shown him that they didn't really know "where Romania is," let alone anything about its history or culture.[16] This worried him. Akhil also felt he wasn't known. He said, "They have no clue what kind of animals are we here, what is our capability, what we can do, what we can't do." You can see why the Americans' claims about valuing equality across the engineers and their statements that "we are all equal" were hard to believe. If you understand the recent histories of Romanians and Indians, you also understand why it's so important to them to be taken into account. Otherwise, it seems to them that old hierarchies still apply—and that they're still at the bottom.

To be fair, each person's cultural history and language background influences them to think in certain patterned ways. This becomes so habitual that everyone tends to assume that the way they hear and make sense is the same for everyone. For example, back in the 1990s, some people enthusiastically predicted that computers and the Internet would lead to the end of hierarchy and create more equal and horizontal lines of communication within every organization. They thought that technology would undermine hierarchical authority,[17] and considered this a positive outcome. Hierarchy, however, is alive and well. Their prediction assumed that every culture would consider the end of hierarchy to be an unmistakably good thing. This prediction was wrong, though. It didn't account for the many cultures in which hierarchies have positive value and need to be maintained, even in the face of technological change.

KNOWING YOUR HEARER

Companies selling products spend a lot of money trying to know their hearers, and advertising isn't something most people even like to listen to! To know who people are, what they want, and why they want it, companies are always observing them.

When business gurus, marketers, and others stress the importance of "knowing your audience," what are they really saying? To some, knowing one's hearers means learning to communicate the way they communicate. It might also mean the related (but different) idea of not forcing them to have to learn your method of communication. Politicians who are elected to office do this all the time when they talk like the people whose votes they are trying to get. So do corporate leaders who make it a point to be accessible to everyone in their companies. But in a global office, you'd have to be a style-shifting chameleon to adapt to all the different cultures and styles—and types of hearers. Copying the style of one's hearer can also indirectly give the message that their social status is higher than yours—a message that might have unintended consequences. So you don't simply want to do that.

We're saying something slightly different. We're not advising that you adjust your accent to match your audience's. We're saying you should know your audience by expecting that they'll have differences in the way they hear—differences you may not be able to identify specifically—and that their listening patterns come from their cultures and histories. We're also saying you should learn about your hearers (rather than presuming things about them) and get explicit and continual feedback from them. We'll emphasize these strategies in the rest of this chapter.

The time crunch in getting a project up and running meant the engineers we studied didn't have time to modify the documents that had already been written with only one type of hearer in mind. This is a common problem. One hot day in Houston, we sat talking with Dave. "Sure," he told us, "we have communicated the project execution plan to them, but it's written with the understanding that we're all working here in the U.S." Dave realized that the project-execution document assumed readers with a shared background, which left out many types of new hearers. He didn't follow up his statement by saying how their assumptions about a certain type of cultural hearer could be dealt with. This narrowly written document had resulted in a barrage of questions, usually by email, which took a lot of time to answer.

Not knowing your hearer when making plans can lead to other problems, too—like undermining your goals. The Romanian dictator Nicolae Ceaușescu in the 1970s assumed he knew how Romanians would "hear" the American TV show *Dallas* (a soap opera about feuding families in the oil and cattle business). He thought the show would be proof to them that capitalism led to moral decline. He expected the rich, glittery, self-indulgent, dysfunctional Texas family the Ewings to show the decadence of the West and reinforce Communist ideals.[18] The show, however, became an instant hit with Romanians and caused a *"Dallas* mania."[19] Alexandru, who loved the show, said he "dreamt in the eighties to migrate to the U.S." Romanian and American viewers alike loved watching the lavish consumption of luxuries, the betrayals and longings. (When we first introduced ourselves as being from Texas, we were warmly welcomed by the Romanian engineers, who mentioned the show and its place in their popular culture.)

THE MYTH OF THE UNIVERSAL HEARER

The engineers often talked as though some universal engineer-hearer existed. Arjun once said, "An engineer is an engineer." Their training in universal principles of engineering, chemistry, math, and physics led each of them—Arjun, João, Dumitru, and Dave—to think about engineering in a way that they believe is similar and predictable. However, they often left out of the equation the big, unpredictable effects of culture. The one exception was when they referred to unexpected "explosions" between people or "lightning storms" of conflict.

This habit—assuming a universal professional hearer in a work environment—is tough to break. Even though we know that by the end of every baby's first year of life, the baby changes from a universal hearer into a language-specific one,[20] the myth persists. What we mean by a universal hearer is the (mistaken) idea that everyone is the same, that everyone interprets language in the same way. This idea of the universal hearer is promoted by idealistic stories, but it falls apart once a person crosses into other cultural worlds. This is perhaps because people don't realize, until they try to learn another language, how much of the universal sound inventory they've lost. There are plenty of great examples of how each person becomes a cultural hearer. In Japanese the difference between the English sounds of the letters *l* and *r* is not significant in meaning (Japanese has a consonant that sounds as if it's between the two), while in English the difference is significant. But native speakers of Japanese who spent their young lives around Japanese and have learned English as adults have a hard time hearing the acoustic differences between English r and l.[21] Native English speakers have similar experiences with Japanese. The myth of the universal hearer even gets applied to deaf people, strangely enough. Some hearing people will try to interact with deaf people not by visual means such as writing a note, but by talking louder. A Swedish colleague told us that when she first came to the United States, she couldn't understand the difference between the intonation patterns of "uh-huh" (yes) and "uh-uh" (no), which are particles Americans use every day. This is another reason that those speaking global English need to feel it's okay and even necessary to be repetitive and ask for explicit feedback.

Thinking of the hearer as universal led to what Dave called "heartburn and fingerburn," along with rework and even more emails and anxieties due to communication problems. In insidious ways, imagining a universal hearer leads to discrimination, because to the hearer it seems as if we speakers have forgotten their unique humanity or cultural heritage and are therefore making them invisible.

Focusing on the unique hearer might take extra work for the speaker, but it has the advantage of reducing the unpleasant task of doing work over again. Not only are mistakes from not knowing your hearer embarrassing, as in the case of the Romanians' unexpected *Dallas* mania; they're expensive, too. Take an example from marketing. When a well-known international company marketed a stuffed wolf toy (after the wolf in the Little Red Riding Hood story) in China, the name they chose for the toy contained a homophone[22] of a profane Cantonese word meaning "vagina." The toy wolf became an overnight sensation, and it was used by some people as a way to insult male political figures by giving them the toy (or even throwing it at them).[23]

The first step in leaving aside the myth of the universal hearer and becoming aware of the cultural influences on hearers involves gaining greater self-awareness about what's unique about your own cultural environment and some of the ways it constantly affects your hearing. To be self-aware, a person must step outside themselves to view their own habits. This is a skill that takes some developing; as one anthropologist said, it would hardly be fish who discovered the existence of water.[24] Habits take a bit of work to change, since they first have to be recognized, and then made more conscious. However, one advantage of working on a cross-cultural team is that one's culturally unique assumptions (about how the world is supposed to work, like the fish in water) become illuminated just through interacting with people who are different. Consider these lines from a scene between John Wayne (as the character John Bernard Books) and Lauren Bacall (as Bond Rogers) in the film *The Shootist*, when Bacall's character tries to make Wayne's character aware of his profanity.

Wayne's character says, "Damn."

Bacall's character says in reply, "John Bernard, you swear too much."

John Wayne's character says, "The hell I do." It's tempting to think that we're in control of our meaning and how our words matter and that there's no need for taking into account how others hear.

An interesting study of international teaching assistants at U.S. universities showed real benefits from learning self-awareness about how they sounded on the job. At first, although the assistants knew their subject area well, they had a lot of problems becoming aware of why and how their teaching style alienated their students. They had trouble figuring out their American hearers as they lectured in the classroom. For some teaching assistants, the American style of letting students' questions influence what was discussed differed substantially from their own educational experiences.[25] Some said that in their cultures, students wouldn't think of questioning the professor. In the end, the foreign teaching assistants found it most useful to learn to hear themselves and monitor themselves in class, and then evaluate (after class) how what they did compared with other teaching styles. These are techniques of self-monitoring, known to psychologists as *metacognition*. This involves a level of cognitive control of one's own knowledge and strategic learning. The teaching assistants were able to take charge of their own learning when they focused on this process.

The myth of a universal hearer is reflected in a lot of advice about communication, such as how to give criticism—the oft-repeated advice to begin with positives, then put any negatives later. (You've probably heard the metaphor of the sandwich: put criticism between two positive comments.)

Research on persuasion shows something to the contrary: whether the pros or cons are presented first should depend on whether or not the hearer is already aware of the pros and the cons. For a hearer who knows about the cons, giving the positive information first is the right way to go. For a hearer who is aware of both the pros and cons, however, the message is more persuasive if the cons go first and the pros afterward.[26] The rule of thumb (positives before negatives) is sufficient only if you assume that all hearers in all situations hear things in the same way. But evidence about actual audiences shows something quite different.

KNOWING YOURSELF AND YOUR HEARER

Some books on cross-cultural communication advocate developing understandings of hearer differences by categorizing cultures. Is a culture individualist? Collectivist? (This distinction seems to come up frequently, and we'll refer to it ourselves occasionally.) Does the culture have a power-distance idea? Is it concerned with uncertainty avoidance? How does masculinity versus femininity play a part?[27] These lists of traits can be helpful in understanding the range and complexity of difference (because most situations will involve multiple types). And when you build self-awareness, it's helpful to focus on difference. But in the ever-changing global office, many players are members of multiple groups, so keeping a list of all the traits in mind is unlikely. People are very imaginative in the ways they use language, so it's also hard to predict how they might express these various traits.

To become better at knowing the hearer, find out something about the personal history of your hearers. It's especially useful to learn about a person's path of development into adulthood. One way to do this is to ask about experiences in schooling, since formal schooling usually involves interesting experiences and stories unique to each culture, as well as explicit teaching and reflection. Asking the questions that help you understand how a person became a "proper person" in their cultural context is actually a lot easier than trying to find commonalities in a mythical universal human being or remembering all the specific traits of different cultures. We're not saying you should treat each individual individually. We're saying you should recognize that each person is really a historical person.[28] When you do so, you'll recognize the developmental path someone takes to be a hearer.

An important stop on anyone's path is their schooling. Some people were schooled to listen and then reflect. Others were taught that active criticism and heated discussion are the only ways to hear what's really going on.[29] Still others learned by heart, by repeating exactly what they were told. Still others weren't considered to have heard and understood unless they expressed their personal opinion about things. We've gone on at length to show the variety of ways to produce a hearer. Even then, we're not done. What were each hearer's school days like? And what happened after school? We know this all takes time, and time is short in the global office, where collaborators have few overlapping hours together. But it's surprising how even something like showing some knowledge about the geography of the other person's country can generate a basis for building knowledge of the hearer.

When we spoke with a university professor in Romania about some of the cities and countrysides we had visited, she was reminded of her student days at the university. She told us that when she was finishing her university schooling, Elena Ceauşescu (the influential wife of the dictator) suddenly decided there were too many young people in the major cities. She ordered that all graduating young people had to work in the countryside. All of a sudden our informant was sent to a very small town, where she found a job in a computer company. To her horror, she discovered that the company had no computers because the boss had taken them to a neighboring city. Her job had evaporated, but she wasn't allowed to return to her home city. All around her, the gates closed and opportunity disappeared, she told us. Knowing this about a person can help you realize that she might be sensitive about promises that are made without written confirmation, or might want a sense of autonomy when deciding a course of action.

There are some good ways to illustrate the importance of understanding hearer development that go further back in each individual's history, too. The cultural path of development for a middle-class North American child these days (a future engineer, if you will) is very different from the paths we took—Elizabeth in the United States and Sirkka in Finland.

North American parents now use more verbal reasoning and negotiation than in the past, when physical punishment and criticism were an accepted means of ensuring good development. Now physical punishment is thought to be the first step to child abuse in some social classes and ethnic groups.[30] Of course all kids negotiate (skillfully) with parents, but the reasons that parents and grandparents give for their actions shape children and adults into cultural hearers and later contribute to cross-cultural misunderstandings. In a cross-cultural example from different continents, West African parents who moved to Paris disagreed with the way they saw French babies being taught to interact with toys and other objects. The West African parents considered it unhealthy and too tiring for the babies, and the West African mothers worried that the children wouldn't develop good social skills (much like the way some parents worry about the negative impact of video games).[31] To them, toys were for teaching how to share with others rather than for improving independent skills or action schemes. A person's stories of school and other personal stories show the cultural beliefs behind how they became who they are and how they make sense of things.

As we learned, Romanian engineers who were in school during the regime of Nicolae Ceauşescu (1967–89) felt uncertain about their future. The secret police's constant surveillance campaigns stamped out dissent, and people were intimidated by forced entry into homes and offices. The economic scarcity influenced engineering designs, and engineers designed to "use less steel" and other formerly scarce commodities. One might think all those dynamics are stories about the past. Horrible, yes—but ones that don't affect us now. One afternoon in Romania as the sun was dropping low in the sky, we heard the Romanian personal experience of an unstable future echo during a conference call with American engineers. The topic of the call seemed straightforward: Constantin asked whether certain dimensions of the structure currently under design should be the same as a previous project's.

"We already said last week it's the same," Dave answered. His tone showed that he didn't think he should have to say it again, and that he was irritated because Constantin and his team appeared not to be paying attention.

"But I have no confirmation," Constantin said.

Something was going wrong. Dave did just confirm, didn't he? To make it as clear as possible, he confirmed again. "It will be the same," he said, with a more authoritative voice.

"Please send the confirmation," Constantin said. He clearly needed something that he couldn't articulate to Dave, something that Dave couldn't see. *Perhaps he's merely been asking for written confirmation,* one might think. That's easy enough.

But to Dave and his team, someone asks for written confirmation because they don't trust the person who's just given them verbal confirmation, and calling someone's integrity into question is a good way to offend someone. To Constantin, it's a perfectly reasonable thing to ask for, because creating a paper trail is one way to protect yourself when you can't be sure of what's going to happen.

On this particular day, neither set of engineers did the great job Cynthia had done when she tried to see through the others' eyes and hear with their ears. Each side just kept doing and saying the same thing. What would have helped? Perhaps a small acknowledgment that they weren't understanding each other's positions as hearers very well. The subtext of that acknowledgment ("We seem to be at odds with each other") would have communicated something like, "I'm having a hard time sharing your world, and it sounds like you're having a hard time sharing mine. But maybe we can manage it if you recognize something about us." Feedback along those lines would open a door to understanding and, hopefully, communicative success.

THE HEARER'S BIGGEST CHALLENGE: INDIRECTNESS

A big challenge to working with your hearer is the widespread use of indirectness. As we talked about earlier in the book, people often speak indirectly, especially when they're asking for something or asking someone to do something (which happens all the time at work). People are indirect because they want to avoid threatening the other person, since adults feel threatened and annoyed by a loss of autonomy or when being ordered around. In many cultures, speakers cloak their requests and directives in different sorts of disguises. As we also mentioned, these disguises leave it up to the hearer to recognize what's going on—and if you're a native, you do so automatically. The point is that indirectness is *designed* to give the hearer all the work. It's a strategy designed to give even more power to the hearer.

One day, during a model review, Mike was commenting on Arjun's team's part of the design. "You might want to make the area around that support larger," he said at one point. "I would make that higher," he said at another. And at still another point he stopped the motion of turning the model and asked, "What's that pipe doing there?" With these phrases, he was displaying some typical American politeness, to avoid being too direct about wanting someone to change something. Mike had learned that it's not a good idea to order people around, because saying, "Make that area larger," or "Make it higher," or "Move that pipe" would be claiming a superior role. If you didn't know what Mike's strategy was, he might sound as if he's making mere suggestions or banal comments, or expressing curiosity.

Hearers from other cultures, like Arjun and João, might feel that Mike was leaving it up to them as to whether to ignore his ideas or follow them. Following his feedback was optional, at least to them. A few weeks later, Mike realized that a lot had to be redone, because the instructions he thought he had clearly directed to Arjun weren't, in fact, implemented. The Brazilians became puzzled: "Why didn't the Americans say what they wanted?" João said to the Americans. "Give us a checklist next time." Dave and Mike, when they found out they had wrongly interpreted something that was said indirectly by João, got frustrated. Why don't the Brazilians "come out and say things openly?" they asked. Dave said they preferred it if someone was "in our face" direct, rather than what they experienced with Arjun and João: "They all go around the edges for a really long time." Arjun and Akhil accused them of the same thing: "Why are the Americans so maddeningly indirect!"

It's ironic that the formulations "you might" or "I would" don't have the force of directives if you're not used to them, precisely because they offer to the hearer the ability to choose. That offer makes them polite, but it's really a conventional way of being polite when giving an order. Not all cultures give orders in that way, though. Hearing what an indirect utterance is trying to convey is fairly routine in one's own culture,[32] but it becomes difficult when playing the communication game with partners from other cultures.

Remember, the use of indirectness is meant to preserve good relationships. This is why a strategy of "be direct" can be tricky: it takes away a resource that cultures give people to build and maintain relationships—and a highly effective resource at that. Politeness is essential, so finding different ways to say the same thing repeatedly is key, as is asking for explicit feedback. Because "indirect" meanings have become conventionalized for some people, they can even seem direct since they are well understood among members of the same culture. However, they're not transparent to the hearer from another culture. They even seem to show that Americans are anything but straightforward; and that damages the reputations of Americans when other interactions arise.

These are our prescriptions for communicative success in the global office: first, pay close attention to the hearer. Second, remember that indirectness is hard on hearers, and be aware of your own indirectness in the cross-cultural global office. Third, expand and repeat what you want done or what you're asking for. It's true that telling a person *less* is a way of respecting the expertise they have. But when we observed the engineers, we saw many times that telling *more* increased understanding. The working relationship that resulted was a better venue for everyone to display their expertise—and to respect that of others.

HEARING DISAGREEMENT

Different cultural styles for conflict avoidance and conflict resolution also affect whether someone is considered a good hearing partner. Most people try to avoid conflict. Some groups do this by flushing out disagreement in advance by spending a lot of time developing consensus, as is done in Japan. In Brazil, people seek collaborative input along the way by checking in with the group and working collaboratively rather than dividing work up. (Americans are puzzled by this aspect of conflict management and question why it takes Brazilians so long to do something. Of course, this "so long" is relative, since to Brazilians, Japanese colleagues can seem to take "so long." Americans also wonder why Brazilians are so tolerant when meetings seem to get off topic.) Good conflict management, no matter in which culture it's done, recognizes that hearers are important.

Americans are often described as more open to communicating points of disagreement than other groups. Are such generalizations really accurate? Americans are said to expect conflict and to see conflict as an efficient way to solve problems. We aren't sure we agree with this, based on our research and observations of the engineers. The most important point is that you should observe yourself as a hearer and understand your behavior around conflict. Become aware of your own habits as a hearer and a speaker in the case of conflict. If you're hinting at conflict, will it be heard in time for the other person to collaborate in avoiding conflict? Will you hear others' hints about upcoming conflict? So when Bill said to João, "You're losin' me" or "You're movin' too fast," or when there was silence from João or Arjun, these were actions that were intended to communicate or foreshadow disagreement. Foreshadowing is important in managing conflict, because it gives the other side time to take action to avoid or mitigate conflict.

Every group knows that conflict is part of working together. Sometimes the conflict is handled in long meetings to gather consensus before a project proceeds, or through tolerating people getting off track in a meeting, or by invoking a boss–worker hierarchy, or in myriad other ways. Unfortunately, accepted ways of managing disagreement in one culture can increase lines of conflict in others. Since people dislike conflict, disagreement is often hinted at or even done in what looks like an *agreement* form, like the familiar "yes, but." It's something to listen for.

OVERTELL

One of the ways to take seriously and put into practice the concept that the hearer is the most important player is to do what might seem like *over*explaining, or *over*telling. Here's an example of how "overtelling" can work.

One afternoon, the Indian engineers and the American engineers were on a conference call to check a design for a series of pipes to carry the crude petroleum in the plant. The 3-D model was on the screen in front of them, along with a series of tables and notes they would occasionally pull up. On the screen, the pipes were colored blue, yellow, brown, red, and purple. Both sets of engineers were able to see the same computer model at the same time, even though the Americans were in their high-rise office in Houston and the Indians were in their high-rise office in Kolkata. However, as we've discussed, just assuming (without checking) that everyone is interpreting what they're looking at in the same way would be a mistake.

On this afternoon, as Burt and Mike were reviewing the design with Manoj, Burt mentioned to Manoj how to mark a particular type of pipe for leak detection on the computer model. He told him that the correct color for leak detection was "spice brown." Mike, who was also part of the conversation, suddenly laughed and repeated the words *spice brown* in a mocking tone. Burt then replied, in a self-conscious tone, that these names ("spice brown" and others) were in fact rather odd. An American would know that in American culture, when someone uses a name for a color that indicates such fine gradations of the mundane brown, or uses the word *spice* (like something in cooking) to describe a color, that behavior stereotypically could be considered feminine. Mike was making a subtle cultural comment about how incongruous he felt it was for male engineers (they were all men on this call) to be demonstrating erudite color knowledge. But the worlds of culture and gender identity are complex and hard to translate cross-culturally. And Burt didn't try. But he did something that worked very well.

During the laughing exchange between Burt and Mike, Manoj didn't join in the humor, and likely didn't know the relevance of a stereotype about an advanced color palette for stereotypes about gender identity. He just acknowledged the color choice, saying "Okay, okay." The point is that what Burt did next showed attention to the hearer, even though it was very simple. He provided information for Manoj in order to account for Mike's laughing. Mike's remark was quite brief, as jokes often are, and lacked explanation. (Humor dies when it's explained.) Mike had merely repeated the two words, *spice brown*, while laughing, and Burt immediately understood what he was getting at. But Burt also took the time to make the connection for Manoj: he connected Mike's laughter to the "odd" name for the color. He said, "That color, it seems like the oddest thing, I'm tellin' ya." He didn't provide the whole gendered history of American color-term usage for an Indian hearer, but he did make the laughter relevant by explaining its source: something funny about the phrase "spice brown." This was a rare instance where a joke was explained. Believe us when we say that we sat in on many others that weren't, sometimes with disastrous results. Not explaining what's going on to the cross-cultural hearer is risky because hearers might interpret the laughter in the wrong way or be offended by an aside that doesn't include them. Here Burt had his cross-cultural hearer in mind as a critical part of the communication game.

Explaining things that might seem obvious in one's own eyes to cross-cultural hearers avoids negatively arousing the hearer. It turns out that when nonnative speakers hear phrases uttered under the breath, or when they hear colorful asides such as jokes, phrases, idioms, and sayings, they can misinterpret them as offensive.[33] That's because a hearer is always looking for relevance. Why is someone saying something? If they're present for an aside that makes someone else laugh, they tend to think it's relevant to the situation. And if they're not included, they assume it's about them. Given the number of nonnative English speakers in the global office, this is an important dynamic to keep in mind.

FEEDBACK

A lot of communication training, especially in corporate environments, is aimed at improving the speaker's behavior. We've noted as much in this book. But everyone has to become better hearers, too. This means giving more feedback. How much do you understand? How well can you hear? Organizations can develop ways to ensure that hearers' habits are changed as well as those of speakers. Without enough feedback, the engineers told us, they routinely "wasted a bunch of days and a bunch of hours" because they didn't get a clarification.

Let's focus on feedback, which we mentioned at the beginning of the chapter. A lot of what hearers do when people are working face to face is give feedback. Often, it's very visual: head nodding, maintaining eye contact, inclining toward the speaker. When lots of people are meeting at the same place, many can communicate feedback at once, using gazes, nods, and smiles. When work moves from a conventional office setting to a global context that's mediated through conferencing technology, the hearer becomes much less visible, unfortunately. So does much of the feedback hearers have to give to the other participants. Even when people's images are visible, they are more difficult to "read" for the subtle facial cues that speakers rely on. It's hard to see the grimaces or puzzled looks—feedback that can influence the speaker. Despite problems with the hearers' visibility, though, the need for their feedback doesn't go away. And the impact can be large. Even though their feedback can seem insignificant, it's knowledge crucial to other participants that can keep the exchange on track.

In many ways, the communication technology that people rely on now takes away as much as it gives. Global teams are possible only because connecting large groups of people instantaneously is cheap and easy to do. Yet these same technologies reduce the visual, physical, and linguistic cues that participants need from hearers in acts of communication.

Sometimes *how* a hearer gives feedback is just as important as the fact that they do, so it's worth noting that a person's first language, as well as their native model of communication, influences how they will provide feedback as a hearer in their second language. This complicates feedback itself, which can become a source of communication problems as well. For instance, the Americans assumed they were giving positive feedback if they gave no feedback at all. (In other words, to them, no complaint communicates "Job well done.") The Indians and Romanians experienced the no-feedback message of the Americans as criticism. That's because the Romanians wanted "to be in touch and informed." They said, "Our people are looking to know they are doing the right thing." When Indians, Romanians, or Brazilians didn't give feedback to the Americans, the Americans assumed everything was fine. This was an incorrect assumption, as it turns out. Additionally, the engineers told us that the way the U.S. engineers expected feedback to work inadvertently established hierarchy. The U.S. engineers expected junior engineers to take the responsibility for giving feedback on their level of understanding.

One early morning in June as we sat in Houston in the conference room, during the weekly update call with Romania, things got so mixed up in terms of feedback and hearer expectations that one side switched off the microphone for several moments and shut the communication game down entirely. It all started when Dumitru and Alexandru asked Dave for specifications for expected pipeline pressures, which they needed for a design. Dave said they didn't have the information. This wasn't the first time Dumitru and Alexandru had asked for these specs. It wasn't the first time that specs were late in coming from Houston. One common holdup was that Houston got the specs from equipment manufacturers, sometimes located in other countries—which came with its own challenges.

After Dave told the Romanians he didn't have that information, Dumitru suddenly expressed a worry that had been growing in his head. He had started to interpret the lack of information as a deliberate withholding of information. And he gave them this feedback. "I think you have some motivation for not sending to us," we heard him say. There was a silence around the room and glances were exchanged. Dave put his hand over the microphone of the speaker and said to the attendees in the room, "Let it go." Dave had heard Dumitru's allegation as an insult, and was telling everyone not to react as negatively aroused hearers. Unfortunately, they didn't try to see Dumitru's statement from his position or negotiate a better understanding of each other as hearers. They instead made judgments about the uncooperativeness of the other. In this way, a hearer's judgments about the speaker influence what assumptions the hearer makes. Dumitru gave feedback about his worries, but his feedback went nowhere, since it was heard as antagonistic.

Remember that what a person says next in conversation tells you a lot about what they heard. Dumitru's comment indicated that he thought that the relationship between his team and the Americans had deteriorated in some way and that they were being shut out. This was important information for Dave, Mike, and the rest of the American engineers. But they missed it.

When U.S. engineers did actively give and solicit feedback ("You wanna make a comment about that?"), or if they heard that no feedback was forthcoming ("I don't know if you caught that, João," or "We like the way you work"), this proved extremely effective in preventing problems from showing up as a surprise later. Mike was especially skilled at constantly soliciting and giving feedback, monitoring the multiple perspectives and hearer states. He prompted the other engineers on his team to explicitly get feedback to increase the visibility of the hearer's role.

Small but repetitive checks on the hearer, especially in cases of potential cultural blindness inherent in technology, are highly effective. A good strategy, used by one of the groups of engineers we studied, was to actively seek constant explicit feedback from particular individuals ("Arjun, did you get what I meant about the stress calculations?") rather than to broadly ask for questions to confirm specific aspects of the hearer's collaborative understanding. It wasn't effective to say at the beginning of the project: "Any questions, call up your counterpart and talk to them." As with the foreign teaching assistants we talked about earlier, asking questions isn't always a part of some cultural repertoires. Among Indians, a hesitancy to answer the question "Are there any questions?" when it's addressed to a group can result from uncertainty (among those asked the general question) as to which person is entitled or authorized to answer for the whole group, or to say that something more is needed. Here hierarchy comes into play, silently but powerfully affecting the work together. Getting feedback from the hearer was done skillfully by one group of engineers, who were careful to locate specific hearers on the conference call by soliciting feedback individually, asking for personal commitments on affirming or disaffirming what was said. One of the best communicators we observed among the Americans asked individuals questions about problems and understanding. When Akhil had been a silent, invisible participant for a time in a conference-call meeting, he was asked, "Any problems with that, Akhil?" Soliciting feedback takes time, but the time spent is an investment that pays dividends. In conference calls with multiple people, those engineers who made sure the hearers' perspectives gained visibility were considered the best to work with. We don't know for sure, but we expect they were more often tagged for advancement, too. Giving others a sense of your visual actions helps, too: "Let's see, I close that window, and now . . ."

In these last examples—indeed, in most of the examples we have used in this book—you can see how everyone possesses a model of communication provided by their culture, a model that suits their everyday interactions fairly well. However, these models don't provide the resources that people need in order to understand, diagnose, and fix cross-cultural communication challenges, especially those challenges that people in the global office encounter. From what we have seen and heard, effectiveness is a function of learning to treat the hearer as important. To do this, you have to reconsider who is the actual crux of communicative success: not the speaker, but the hearer.

Learning how to do this is a necessary skill in the global workspace, and we'd just like to stress that it is a skill that is possible to learn. The people we witnessed who were communicating effectively by using these techniques had to acquire these skills, since neither their training as engineers nor their native models of communication contained those skills. On an everyday basis, when people are talking with someone from their own cultural group, they can often repair communication problems because everyone shares the same understandings of what goes wrong and why.[34] They also share the same resources for fixing them. In cross-cultural communications, people don't share that same sense of when something has gone awry or how to fix it. You have to acquire an explicit model of communication for these cross-cultural exchanges, one that includes thinking of the hearer as the most important player. How the hearer interprets has to be part of the idea of getting it "correct." Treat the hearer as central, expect differences in hearing, and get feedback from hearers on their understanding.

The bright spot is that knowing your hearer and giving them an important role enables you to better predict and control what happens next.

4 How to Make Their Jokes Funny

(HINT: IT'S THE COMMON GROUND)

Most of us have experienced what happens when someone from another culture, generation, or profession tells their favorite joke but we don't get it. It doesn't make us laugh. Why are jokes hilarious only to those with a certain background, and why does humor translate so poorly? Consider the following joke:

> Tortoise is at a party for a wedding, and there's mashed yams on the stove. He's wearing a hat, so he goes to the kitchen and says hi, scoops some yams into the hat, and goes outside to take it home, thinking he's going to eat it. A few minutes later, the other guests find him, and he's lying on the ground in pain. They are like, "Oh, what's wrong with Tortoise?" They check his legs, they check his arms, they check his shell, and they say, he's so sweaty, why is he so sweaty? And someone says, "Take off his hat!" So they take off his hat, see the yams, and say, "He came for the food! That's why he's here!"

This joke is about Tortoise, a favorite character in Nigeria (mostly in the Yoruba, Igbo, and Edo-Bini cultures), where the joke is considered quite funny.[1] If you didn't laugh or even chuckle, even though you read it in English, don't worry: local jokes don't translate into the English of the global office very well, in the same way that global English is ill-equipped to preserve the humor of jokes that come from other languages. The engineers liked to joke while working, making the job more fun. But their jokes usually misfired. One morning when we were all sitting around the conference table, Dumitru (phoning in from across the world) made a joke about something Cynthia had said about email.

"I was gonna send you an email," Cynthia said.

"I haven't gotten any email," Dumitru said, laughing.

"Dumitru, Dumitru, I said . . . ," Cynthia protested.

Even though Dumitru was laughing, Cynthia didn't get his joke. He was taking off from a Communist-era joke that refers to how people adapted to broken promises: "They [the employers] pretend to pay us," the joke goes, "so we [the employees] pretend to work." Dumitru's joking here is a kind of wry comment that business hasn't changed very much. Cynthia and Dumitru never closed the loop on this joke, and the opportunity for lightheartedness was missed. The joke contributed instead to Cynthia's feeling that Dumitru wasn't focused enough on the difficult communication process and that he even made it harder at times. For Dumitru's part, the missed opportunity to share in humor contributed to his opinion that Americans weren't interested in being friendly.

Jokes depend completely on whether the joker and the listeners share notions about what makes something funny and what behavior people can be teased about. This shared background goes by the term *common ground* in cognitive science,[2] social psychology, and linguistic anthropology, where it refers to the way in which people take certain cultural knowledge and put it into action. We happen to have spent a lot of time watching Dave, João, Arjun, and Dumitru dance around the holes in their common ground—their knowledge about how people commonly behave and are supposed to behave (including in joke telling and appreciation of jokes).

Common ground makes it possible to work with others and to be playful with others, and, even more important, to predict what is likely to happen next. You can predict what other people are likely to do because you are—to take the phrase *common ground* at its most literal—standing in the same place. We're going to expand this idea of how humor depends on common ground to talk about how common ground has to be present in every conversation, and how you can build common ground.

Jokes are complex: there's the expectation set up initially, and then a twist or rupture in people's expectations, which gets the laugh. Jokes disrupt hearers' predictions, and people laugh at these unexpected reversals. Take the joke "I went to a fight the other night and a hockey game broke out." Even though this is certainly a bizarre image of a sports event, it works because of common ground (i.e., everyone in certain cultures knows that fights are common at hockey games), and it also shatters people's automatic expectations about what might happen at a fight, and then creates an amusing surprise. Unfortunately, shattered expectations aren't as amusing in the global office. As Constantin said, because multiple cultures are present in the global office, it can seem like "everything comes as a surprise," and "it's hard" to know what to expect and what's expected.

Common ground is necessary for hearers to get jokes because how things are *supposed* to go or usually go is fertile ground for playing with audiences. Take the following joke about people in a bar and the dating scene, and a "cheesy" (cheap and inauthentic) pickup line: "This guy said to this young woman in a bar, 'I think you're suffering from a lack of vitamin me.'" The joke depends on familiarity with the common bar scene, and knowledge of Americans' self-involvement and self-promotion tendencies. It also draws on knowledge about the similar sounds of "vitamin me" and "vitamin E," the latter of which is highly promoted for its heart-protective function, among other things. The phrase "suffering from" helps the joke work because it's a phrase used ad nauseam by advertisers promoting cures. None of this knowledge is provided in the joke, and the teller won't add it, either. It's stuff that hearers have to already know.

Even though "common ground" might sound like it's a physical thing or place, it's invisible. Its invisibility is one reason that establishing common ground in a global office is difficult and at times frustrating to achieve.[3] A survey of fifteen thousand managers from twenty-eight countries over a ten-year period[4] found that people struggled because of unshared common backgrounds, and had difficulties getting to the tacit cultural knowledge that forms common ground and that people use in everyday settings. The absence of this knowledge was difficult to cope with.[5] The managers said they were surprised at the extent to which culture influenced people's actions in ways that aren't seeable. And even though it's true that we started by talking about common ground in jokes, we'll discuss coping with common-ground differences in many types of interactions.

Anthropologists like Elizabeth are trained to believe that people can't describe their own tacit knowledge. The implication is that people know more than they can tell.[6] What people say is that they do things "the way they've always been done." Their responses seem automatic to them, and they've never thought about them. Take the famous aphorism that if your only tool is a hammer, you see every problem as a nail. People don't expect hammers (or their wielders) to be able to articulate what they sense, intuit, or automatically do when they encounter nails. It's the same with people, by and large. Most people *do* their tacit knowledge; they don't talk about it. This becomes a loop: tacit knowledge grows through doing things, and shared experiences with others constantly shape common behavioral knowledge about how to do things and get things done.[7] One consequence of the loop is that rule making and rule following (as Lee suggested about communication in chapter 1) are difficult, because rules are *explicit* expressions of knowledge, and a lot of knowledge is tacit—embodied habit.[8]

The engineers showed us that lack of common ground caused mistakes in the global office for several reasons.[9] One is that common ground is highly dependent on local experiences, behavior patterns, and expectations. A second is that operating as a professional in many different parts of the world requires people to use background knowledge that's different from what they're used to, but actually (because of habit) people misapply knowledge of common ground from one setting to another—from, say, a local setting to a global one. A third, and perhaps the most important, is that people find it challenging to build new common ground in the moment and to recover from common-ground mismatches.

To deal with invisible differences in background knowledge, people first have to recognize the role of common ground in communication. Working against people is that they don't notice common ground in their own cultures, so it's hard for them to recognize it elsewhere. For the purposes of this chapter, what we do have, however, are three ways that anyone from any culture can use to make common ground visible: we talk about *schemas, scripts,* and *frames.*

SCHEMAS, SCRIPTS AND FRAMES: BACKGROUND
KNOWLEDGE

Cognitive scientists, psychologists, and those solving artificial-intelligence problems make common ground visible so they can analyze how it works. They do this by identifying several aspects of common ground, the most relevant of which, to our discussion of the global office, are *schemas*, *scripts*, and *frames*. These three aspects of common ground are in some ways similar and in some ways different. (They actually come from three different stages in research to understand human and machine thinking). Schemas are sets of ideas that help people organize everyday input from others and their surroundings—sort of general theories about what people do and why, their regular patterns of behavior (social roles, activity types, etc.).[10] These patterns (stereotypical patterns, if you will) are seen over and over, and all members of a culture learn to recognize and respond to them.

An interesting study many years ago showed schemas to be so important that they influenced the way people recalled things. The research showed how culture influenced recall.[11] In the research, people from different cultures all read the same story, a Native American folktale, "The War of the Ghosts," and then were asked about details of the story later, even a year later. It turned out that when people retold the story, they changed certain details of the story so that the story was more in line with their own cultural schemas and expectations.[12] They even altered the order of events, the story's emphasis, and its style. Researchers noticed that if some part of the folktale didn't make sense according to a person's own cultural norms and expectations, the person added material to the story. This means that memories are influenced by cultural schemas, which in turn influence what people consider plausible. A person's schemas are resistant to change, too, because people tend to use new information to support their schemas rather than to disprove them.[13]

People not only develop schemas about the world; they also learn and share *scripts*, such as "how to order in a restaurant" and "how to take an exam in engineering school."[14] Of course, such scripts are never written out, but people perform social encounters as if they were actors who knew their lines and knew each other's parts. One script that we had to learn (when we were doing the research for this book in Romania) was "how to pay your fare on the bus"; having made a wrong assumption initially, we were generously given prepaid bus tickets by other passengers. (Clearly they were using another script—one of generosity to hapless strangers.) To a Nigerian, the scripts in the tortoise joke will seem familiar: what guests usually do at wedding parties, how food is usually offered, how people jump to help someone in distress. Tortoise, a greedy guest, gets trapped embarrassingly by his own selfishness. These sequences become part of common-ground knowledge.

Some of the schemas operating in the engineering world were like stories, like the life history of an engineering design. And chapters in the story were scripts like "how to do model review" (where engineers looked together at a computer model of pipes and machines of the processing plant and commented on it). Even though the engineers were similarly trained, the way they conducted the multiple activities that went into all the phases of an engineering design were surprisingly different, as they found at those times when they had to stop and explain things in order to help others make sense, or when a mistake caused days of backtracking.

Anthropologists also use the term *frames*[15] to make visible another important aspect of how people build common ground. In the same way that people have scripts for doing things (like model review and paying the fare on a bus) and people have schemas that are generalized theories of how people behave, they have frames that they use to interpret what's going on and what other people are up to at a particular place or time. When you come across two people doing something together that looks familiar, acting out social scripts, how do you know whether you're witnessing a legal dispute or a commercial exchange? When you come into a room, how do you know whether it's a classroom or an office? There are recognizable ways people are behaving and talking and using space and objects that *frame* what's going on as an activity that's different from surrounding activities.[16] It's worth noting that a lot of these recognizable patterns are nonverbal, too (including physical behavior and posture, seating arrangements, and objects).[17] Different office environments cue an "office" frame in different ways.

People use frames to interpret and take part in many types of activities and life events, including the life passages the engineers didn't have much chance to talk about in their conference calls, such as weddings and funerals. A wedding frame includes those aspects of a scene that let you recognize that a wedding is going on and what to expect when it's starting, how long it will last, and when it will end. In the Tortoise joke, the wedding frame, if we're Nigerian guests, tells us what's expected and how to dress, what the sequence of actions will be, and how to interpret them. (Part of the humor of that joke is that Tortoise breaks the wedding frame.) People's behavior gives signals about the frame and what kind of activity is going on. The environment acts as a signal, too.[18]

People use frames every day, to show at work that coffee or tea break time has arrived, or that we're in a conference call, a meeting, or an interview. And people use frames to know which scripts to use, and how to comport themselves in that context. Speakers also use frames when they join something already happening or want to start something new. Jokes set up a frame (of reference), and then hearers build expectations around the frame that is in play in the joke. But then the joke teller subverts hearers' expectations by providing a new "punch line" frame of reference. Laughter comes from the fact that the new framing can in fact coexist with the hearer's initial frame. An example is the joke "Where does George Washington keep his armies?" (With this framing, the hearer thinks: eighteenth-century American history, battles, and barracks.) The answer is "In his sleevies." (It's a pun on *arms* and *sleeves,* and works because both frames—history and the body—can be correct at the same time.)[19]

People's knowledge of cultural frames gives them the power to predict the future or what's likely to happen next (except when someone switches frames on us and we find we're surprised in a joke) by providing a framework for what's likely to happen next. For example, when we went with the engineers to a company party and cricket match in the countryside of India, we saw that no one talked about stress loads in pipes or equipment foundations. Such topics weren't part of the frame. Instead, new scripts, like what it takes to be a good wicket keeper in cricket or who's the best bowler, became available.

People sometimes invoke a frame verbally, such as when they begin a joke by saying, "Did you hear the one about?" or "Two guys walk into a bar . . ." People use their knowledge of frames to predict what's going to happen next. For example, when theatergoers see the lights in the theater dim, they quiet down and shift in their seats as a response to the visual cue, and their shifting in their seats becomes another visual cue to others that the frame is shifting. Something else is about to happen! (In the global office, the nonverbal signals that people use to frame activities and interpret them are largely invisible to others who are sharing the same social space. This makes being explicit about common ground even more important.)

We recall the time that Dave said, "Okay, let's get started," using an explicit frame cue that indicated that the conference call meeting had begun. Arjun told us that sometimes he and his colleagues were annoyed when part of the American engineering team continued conversations on the side after the conference call had started. It was like sitting in front of people who talk during a movie; concentration becomes more difficult, and you're faced with the effrontery of people who insist on occupying a different frame. It's hard to make sense and know what to do next when there are competing frames. When the engineers continued having side conversations, it could imply that those in Houston have more power, because they're in control of when the meeting really starts and can keep others guessing.[20]

The frame idea is built on the visual metaphor of a picture frame, which indicates something separated off, something to be seen differently than its surrounding environment. The idea of the frame came from scientists trying to understand how to build a machine intelligent enough to do what people do seemingly without even thinking (categorize new information and make sense of it within what they already know). People's ability to see and use frames, scripts, and schemas is remarkable and quite taken for granted, like a lot of their native communication skills.

Sometimes you know you have a cultural difference in schemas and frames because people keep asking you the same questions again and again. If a question seems to be one that you thought you'd already answered multiple times, your answer wasn't plausible within the cultural schemas of the hearer. Another example from Pohnpei can show how this plays out. The Pohnpeians kept asking Elizabeth why she had come to their small, remote island to study them. "We know that no one is really interested in us," they told her. She explained to them about anthropology, and the importance of studying the range of human diversity, no matter the size of the place. She told them she was interested in language and hierarchy and that their island's intricate system of social status made it an ideal research site. Still, they kept asking her why she was there. One day, having used up her ideas about how to answer or how to account for the Western preoccupation with collecting data around the world, she said, "My dissertation supervisor told me I had to come here." And they nodded understandingly, and that was the end of that question, because in Pohnpei when someone higher up on the chain tells you to do something, it doesn't have to make sense on its own.

Returning to the engineers, common ground has to be established among the different cultural histories, too, so the engineers can make sense of each other's actions. "If you don't understand something, just ask me," Bob said to Rajesh. Bob's credibility was based on his words making sense to Rajesh, but others heard his words according to their own contexts. When he said this, he was using an American sort of schema, where a person who asks questions signals their active engagement. He's predicted that if Rajesh has any questions, he'll ask. But Rajesh doesn't ask questions easily. To him, a question lands in a different sort of common ground. In India, asking questions signals that you don't know what you should know. You lose credibility. (To be honest, it's difficult for everyone to admit they aren't following in a professional context.) Or it could be you don't think it's your role to ask questions; maybe that's something only the boss is supposed to do in these group settings.

Sometimes when people think they stand on common ground, they'll find that they don't share what they thought they did. We can see an example of this if we step away again from engineering briefly and look at an example of how shared knowledge of the world can seem to be similar but isn't. Although this is an example about children, we thought it was especially good for showing the complexities behind imagining someone else's point of view and how hard it is to know if you're on common ground. The example is as follows: Some researchers asked six-year old children around the world what shape the world was. Almost all the children said that the earth is a circle or round. A preliminary conclusion might be that their ideas were similar. But when the researchers asked the children to draw the earth or to make clay models of it, they found a surprising difference. For many of the children, a round earth meant something circular but flat, like a disk, that people lived on. For other children, people lived inside a round sphere, not on it. Still others believed there are two earths: a flat one people live on, and a round one in the sky.[21] This is perhaps an extreme example, but it shows the importance of not making assumptions too early or too simply about common ground.

Cultural assumptions and expectations unfortunately resist new framing and new schemas. Anthropologists learn this, too, when they're in the field—how hard it is to change one's assumptions. In Elizabeth's fieldwork in Pohnpei, she encountered new schemas, scripts, and frames and discovered the great distance between knowing that a person's cultural perspective transforms what they see in front of them and becoming aware of the *ways* in which their cultural perspective is transforming what's really there. Her own cultural frames, including the work of being an anthropologist, were unrecognizable and puzzling to the Pohnpeians she lived with. Spending time alone writing notes and reading were considered unfriendly and antisocial behavior there. Elizabeth didn't know at first that the cultural script for sharing a meal was that people ate in hierarchical order, not at the same time. Other foreigners had shown a similar ignorance about the local views on mealtime, not realizing that in Pohnpei all the food is served to the highest-ranking person present; then, when they're finished eating, all the food left is served to the next-ranking person; and so on down the line. Some foreigners told Elizabeth about following their own cultural script of "Eat everything your host serves you" (clean your plate). They were later very embarrassed to learn that no one else got anything to eat, since they finished it all. Imagine the dismay of all those lower-status people and children who had waited respectfully with gnawing stomachs!

Such mismatches of frames, scripts, and schemas cause confusion and embarrassment and trigger resentment. If people have a positive attitude, though, even mismatches can lead to a better understanding of scripts or frames (and even provide material for jokes). The Pohnpeians never lost an opportunity to joke and laugh about embarrassing moments. One embarrassing moment they enjoyed retelling was the time Elizabeth used an impolite greeting to the paramount chief. The paramount chieftainess and secondary chieftainess were instructing Elizabeth every day on different aspects of Pohnpeian culture, and at this point they told her, "Go say good day to the paramount chief"; they said, "*Kohla nda rahnmwahu Mwohnsapwko*,"—instructions that Elizabeth took too literally. Elizabeth went to the chief and said, "*rahnmwahu Mwohnsapwko*," repeating exactly what was modeled, as learners do in the cultural script from home. It turns out that the second word (*Mwohnsapwko*) was very respectful ("First of the Land"), but that in repeating the first word (*rahnmwahu*) exactly from the words the chieftainess used as "good day" (and being so confident that it translated literally in her head to a rather formal English "good day"!), Elizabeth ended up importing to the situation her own common ground about what sounded respectful. As it turned out, what she repeated wasn't a real greeting at all, but rather the instruction to "greet" someone. So what she really conveyed in respect terms toward the paramount chief probably came out something like "Hey there, O First of the Land." The incongruity (mismatched frames) was hilarious to everyone there.

So common ground helps predict what might happen next through familiar scripts, schemas, and frames. The chieftainess expected Elizabeth to share more common ground at that point about how to greet (there were different greetings for different statuses of people), and Elizabeth used her U.S. schema: how people told you exactly what to say in certain formal situations when they were teaching their language. Cross-cultural situations, though, can seem unintuitive, as some have described it, when the unexpected happens. One U.S. airline found this out when it started to offshore accounting work and had to make "unintuitive" (or so it seemed to them) adaptations in the work process in order to accommodate cultural variation. At first, the airline had assumed that its accounting operations lacked cultural content (since these operations all involved math).[22] To the airline, accounting and the scripts around reporting regulations were surely so clear-cut as to be culturally neutral (or so it thought). To the airline's credit, once the differences were noticed, it learned more about the offshore group's cultural background and expectations, then changed its procedures.[23] Eventually, the company even adapted its model of quality control to the local culture by making the scripts for quality checking less hierarchical. It also accommodated the employees' desire to integrate both home and work lives into the company's quality-control concepts. This better fit the local cultural schema of consistency in practices across home and work.

Let's return to the engineering offices, where there was little chance to meet chiefs or greet royalty face to face. There, the engineers also had issues in finding common ground. When Cynthia and Dave were slightly embarrassed and needed to apologize to Andreea for not having sent a drawing she asked for, they used a common U.S. schema for apologies (apologize for keeping someone waiting) and (common to them) script. They told Andreea, as they often did, how busy they were. This "being busy" builds common ground among Americans. (Strangely, Americans' everyday chit-chat often concerns sharing how busy they are.) This is something that people from other cultures find strange and even impolite, as was the experience of one visitor to Texas:

> One of the things I've noticed is how busy you lot are. Or at least think you are. Everyone I've met in Texas, it's always "I've got to go to this" or "I'm late to that" or "I don't have time for that." You all love talking about how busy you are. I find it irritating more than anything, to be honest. It's like they're trying to impress me by how busy they are. And really, I don't care how busy you are.

For Americans, talking about how busy they are can be a way of gaining social status or claiming self-importance, and it also has just become a habit for answering the question "How are you?" Being busy can't be used to build common ground cross-culturally. In fact, it can undo common ground. But it's easy to label someone as difficult or incomprehensible without trying to understand their different frames of interpretation.

Building common ground by understanding schemas, scripts, and frames takes time in cross-cultural situations. But it's an important investment in the future of any project. Dan expressed this well. He said everyone had to learn to see what the other sees. Unfortunately, *when* people learn about common ground matters, too. Dan wishes they'd known some things sooner. He wishes they'd realized earlier that their initial predictions about some engineers' behavior were wrong. "We collected many things at a later stage," he lamented. In one sense, it did no good to wish that other engineers had shared more common ground and had interpreted their instructions and requests differently. The moment had passed; the damage was done. In another sense, perhaps they'd get to use their knowledge in the future. People build up new assumptions about those in other cultural groups based on both failed and successful encounters. Both generate expectations about how people are supposed to behave. The engineers' continued interactions helped to build more common ground over time.[24]

As some of the engineers encountered "unintuitive" outcomes—mistakes, setbacks, and misunderstandings due to unique cultural common ground—they tried to make the other engineers more like them, which implied that the former were trying to get the latter to ignore their own cultural backgrounds and adopt new cultural assumptions. Americans gave engineers from other cultures engineering manuals and written descriptions, while Romanians tried to get the Americans to accept communication by hierarchy. But these kinds of cultural transformations are fantasies. The complex knowledge that makes up common ground is hard to itemize. "There is not a book that says, 'Read this and you'll know,'" Mike told us. He'd recognized that common ground isn't built through explanations. It's not built through rules. *It's built through carefully observing others and taking part in activities with them.* Meanwhile, the Romanians had realized that their love of hierarchy, while sustainable in other contexts, was a barrier, given the geographical separation and differing cultural attitudes about hierarchy. Both sets of engineers ended up adapting to a hybrid form that included a chain-of-command approach along with peer-to-peer contact. The flexibility of both sides helped to counter the irritation that flared when expectations weren't met or predictions about work flow were wrong. Here's the good news: as that relationship showed, common ground builds over time.

CORRECTLY PREDICTING WHAT WILL HAPPEN NEXT

When someone correctly predicts what's going to be said next, neuroscientists have shown that their brain activity is similar, at that very moment, to the brain activity of the person whose actions and speech they are predicting.[25] The neuroscientists were studying short strings of words in highly predictable contexts and looking only at which linguistic elements hearers predicted would come next; but the research highlights the way hearers' brain activity is more similar to that of speakers when they are able to correctly predict what a speaker is going to say next. Their predictions are based on their cultural experience, and on their own habits of speaking and hearing. Engineers from the same culture can more easily anticipate what might happen next in routine interactions based on long experience with familiar patterns, including schemas, scripts, and frames. There is already a great deal of common ground. Others who have had different cultural experiences with patterns of speaking, however, have different habits and predictions.

How might this affect a conversation in the global office? For instance, when Americans hear a pause, or delay, or something like "Well . . ." in answer to a yes/no question, they can be fairly certain that the answer is going to be an answer that the other person thinks they won't like. People delay the bad news or formulate it carefully. This happens so frequently that Americans are able to predict a yes or no answer just by the pause or someone starting an answer with "Well . . ." But this assumption about what comes after a delay won't necessarily be shared by speakers who don't share the same cultural background. In some places it's common to pause before *every* answer. So one engineer might have thought he was preparing another engineer for a negative answer by delaying,[26] while actually the hearer just assumed he was being thoughtful and respectful (which is true, too, because giving negative answers has to be done with more care than saying yes). When hearers predict what another person is going to say or do next, their brains can work more quickly, as neuroscientists have shown. The brain sends a signal to the auditory cortex to expect sound patterns of predicted words.

You could think of scripts, schemas, and frames as ways in which people give signals to others and in which others interpret them to make judgments and predictions. In the case of jokes, the predictions fail (because the frame is switched by the joke teller at the end), and that's what's fun. When Dave, Dumitru, Arjun, and João overassumed common ground, though, and their predictions failed, expensive mistakes occurred. One side misread how the other team would behave or how they'd interpreted something, because they hadn't yet built enough common ground. It led Rajesh to say about the U.S. engineers: "There are probably some language barriers and some foreign cultural barriers, so I think it's a combination of all of this that is probably working *in their background.*"

Rajesh's computational metaphor (about some process working in the background) could lead to the assumption that lack of common ground could be fixed by changing background processing. But we know that people have to establish and reestablish common ground all the time.

What people know about common ground, particularly how much has been established at any particular point, is partly a function of cues and patterns they've learned over a lifetime. Also, it's partly a flexible reaction of applying that knowledge to what's happening in front of them. The knowledge they have allows them to guess where the other person is going (both literally and figuratively) and what they want to do. This makes teamwork possible. Sometimes, as we know, these predictions can be proved wrong, even in a person's own cultural group. Expecting common-ground differences is reasonable. We can predict there will be common-ground issues!

BUILDING UP COMMON GROUND IN THE MOMENT AND FIXING COMMON-GROUND MISTAKES

We're always working on establishing common ground. Miss Dimple and Chico, two characters used by some cognitive scientists to illustrate common ground, show this as follows:

MISS DIMPLE: Where can I get a hold of you?

CHICO: I don't know, lady. You see, I'm very ticklish.

MISS DIMPLE: I mean, where do you live?

CHICO: I live with my brother.[27]

Miss Dimple's "I mean" is one way you can see a speaker working at fixing or repairing common ground. She's first used an idiom that left some room for ambiguity ("get a hold," a colloquial expression), and Chico exploited that. They are not on the same page (to use an idiom!), but they are able to fix it and get back on track. A simple example from the engineers shows this, too.

Dave said, "Yeah, I know, I know, okay. Okay, we'll discuss it and try to send some email or something to you."

Don added, "It'll be," then he paused, "later today."

"Okay!" Dumitru said.

Then Dave added, "Your tomorrow then."

And Don agreed with the correction, "Okay . . . which, which is your tomorrow, right."

The best engineers at communicating in the global office used language and questions to clarify common-ground issues and make sure they were on the same page. One morning on a conference call, for example, Don started to tell Rajesh how to proceed. "What you need to do is take a markup of the PNID for that and mark up the way you were told to do it," he said. "Send that off to David and say . . ."

At that point, Rajesh interrupted. "David Smith," he said. By saying David's last name, he was making sure they were talking about the same person. He wanted to make sure he had correctly predicted which David was meant to get the drawings.

"David Smith," Don confirmed, then continued: ". . . that the PNID doesn't match the directions we were given. Here's the markup to make it match, and please issue a DI or tell me to go with what the PNID has." These are very simple examples of building common ground. If you blink, they might pass you by. But if this building isn't done, expensive errors will be inevitable.

On another day, Cynthia, Dumitru, and Andreea were trying to come to some agreement about the parameters of a certain decision. Cynthia said to the other two: "I think that will be the right thing to do, but I want to make sure which system we were talking about in dates here." The *that* ("I think *that* will be the right thing") represents common ground they've already worked out. However, they're still not sure that they're on the same page about systems and dates. They react to the immediate situation that is developing. Unfortunately, much of their individual cultural knowledge remains invisible and is never explicitly brought into the interaction. In this case, Cynthia didn't mention that she wanted to check if European dates (day/month) or American dates (month/day) were being used. This could affect delivery promises in big ways.

Understanding and learning about others' common ground and constantly checking "ground" is especially important in the computer-mediated cross-cultural office. Common-ground problems are fixable, as we know from the times we've said or heard, "Oh, *that's* what you were talking about." Late one afternoon as we were in Romania, observing the engineers there, we heard the following case of unexpected dissonance in understanding what a progress report means.

"You want this progress report in our report," Constantin was saying, "which we send to Tiffany, the pressure and cost-control report—"

"Well, cost control is not really an engineering status report," Dave began, and after a long pause added, "is the problem."

"I understand," Constantin said.

It was an important moment. Both men had just revealed to each other that they didn't share common ground. Couldn't they stop to align ideas about weekly reports and supply each other with background knowledge? They could have. But they didn't, and the conversation moved on. They treated it as a *simple* common-ground matter, something more easily fixed (like Miss Dimple and Chico did), but it was more complex than that. Why is cost control not really an engineering status report? It turns out that review of a job status is only the first step in a project control report. This is a difference in schema or general theories of engineering reporting. The potentially huge implications of common ground about reporting were underlined when Cynthia said, "Unless I have a weekly update of your progress, I cannot regularly report the progress on this project." When engineers don't share common ground about what belongs in an engineering status report, that's going to hold Cynthia up, and perhaps the trajectory of the entire project as well.

As we just saw, the fact that Dave and Constantin both speak English wasn't enough to ensure that common ground would be built. But English *can* be used to develop common ground, not only in the present, but by taking time to look at national histories and other common grounds of those on the cross-cultural team. We talk more about this in chapter 5.

The companies that Dave, Dumitru, João, and Rajesh worked for were aiming to split up a big engineering job into smaller components. This constantly required in-the-moment common-ground checking to be able to anticipate how the various parts were designed to relate, because problems quickly rippled across the whole project. As Arjun described it: "There's a lot of these technical messages going back and forth, telling people what to do and what they did wrong and what they left out: 'When you do this, you're supposed to do that.' So, that's all good. But there's hundreds of them out there. Lots of information. Lots of information."

What this means is that a tremendous amount of learning has already gone on—an amount of learning that is easy to underestimate, especially in the global work setting. There people tend to focus on the mistakes or nerve-racking surprises. People don't tend to give their colleagues credit for the work they're doing.

Building common ground is constant, but people are so used to it in their own culture that they don't notice when they do it. Yet it has to be seen as an important part of the job in the global office. After another early-morning call in the United States, Mike gave a good example of how frames can differ when he told us about a problem he had with some drawings Andreea sent. The drawings were puzzling because they weren't what he expected to receive.

Mike said: "If it was somebody upstairs, I would have just walked up and told them what's going on and wouldn't have to sit down and write detailed item-by-item email, but it was a lost-in-translation type of situation. It's invariably going to happen at some level just because of our lack of familiarity with their culture. Probably the way we relate to our peers is not the same way they do." What really puzzled Mike was how the other engineers never raised a question. "If they didn't get any document, they should've raised a question, like, 'Hey we didn't get all the ones you listed, is it a problem?' No, they went and plugged that gap with whatever they thought we said instead of trying to clarify."

Here Mike might have problem-solved a bit about the different schemas and scripts for getting clarification in different cultures and the role that questions play in each, habits that may frame uncertainties in varied ways and ways he's not used to. He might have also asserted the need for professionals in the global office to actively check understanding at every point. One engineering team we observed did an excellent job of constantly checking common ground, and they framed their repeated requests for feedback in tactful ways.

Building common ground is easier when people hang out together. Andreea was puzzled about why she was reminded to attend a certain meeting while she was visiting the team in Houston. "It was not for me," she said. To her, the discussion of man-hours was not relevant in her schema about her role, since "the budget is not my job." But if she hadn't gone to the meeting, she would have missed a good opportunity to learn about how others built common ground—and to actually build common ground, to be used later. She would have seen scripts and frames in action.

We sometimes saw the engineers react to problems with common ground with incredulity and antagonistic attitudes. The engineers treated different and unexpected schemas, scripts, and frames as intentional slights and offenses.

METAPHORS BUILD NEW COMMON GROUND, OR DO THEY?

Metaphors are a powerful way people create common ground. They are like jokes, though, because they assume a lot of cultural knowledge. Metaphors are powerful because they link something that's hard to explain to something easily found in people's everyday experience.[28] Scientists are always searching for a good metaphor to explain difficult concepts and build common ground in terms of nonscientists' everyday experiences. It was a challenge to create a metaphor to explain the Higgs boson particle, something no scientist had ever seen or documented. But scientists came up with a metaphor to describe this particle that imparts mass to other particles. The metaphor involves three real people (a famous person, a professor with exams to hand out, and an unknown person) who were moving through a crowd. Each person (the famous one, the one handing out exams, and the unknown one) differently attracted attention. And the different ways they attracted attention were metaphorically used by the scientists as a stand-in for a particle attracting mass. People invent communication metaphors, too (but both scientists and communicators can also create bad metaphors, like the computer metaphor for communication). Remember how the engineers often talked about communication as a physical transfer? "Let's see if I can get this across to you," they'd say. This metaphor—of communication as a conduit of information—led them to predict that if they were more direct, they could overcome their communication difficulties. (The prediction was incorrect, as it turns out—a bad metaphor.)

Although metaphors and other imaginative ways of speaking like idioms can powerfully enhance communication, they can also be lost on cross-cultural hearers, like jokes. All the engineers knew that metaphorical speech and idioms caused problems in understanding in the global office, but they had a hard time not using them. The project controls manager in Houston was jokingly referred to as "Mr. Slang himself" because he used so many idiomatic and metaphorical expressions. In one conference call when they were discussing the layout of the petroleum plant, there was uncertainty about whether a valve placement should be changed. Mr. Slang said, "We need to be able to paint a big brush on this thing." He meant they should look at the issue more broadly. We also heard him use phrases like "You're the fly on the wall," and "Mike is going to weigh in on this, too." The others didn't have the shared background to understand these colorful ways of talking.

Once when we were sitting in on a conference call between the United States and Romania, Cynthia said to Dumitru: "Now that you're working *full-fledged* on this project, I need a weekly report from Romania on your weekly activities from Romania." To be working *full-fledged* means to be fully equal members of the team—an important milestone for any group. Cynthia was recognizing this achievement. But the rest of the interaction didn't go well. At first, Dumitru hedged. Constantin is busy, he said. Then he capitulated: "Starting from next Monday, you'll start to receive this report."

But this wasn't acceptable to Cynthia. "Not starting next Monday," she said. "Starting this Friday." There was a long pause.

Then Dumitru made an agreement sound like "Mmmhmm." Cynthia explained: "Because more and more work is going to be done in Romania and less and less in Houston, and unless I have a weekly update of your progress, I cannot regularly report the progress on this project."

Finally Dumitru agreed. "Okay," he said.

Cynthia had said "full-fledged" to point out they had graduated. She likely intended to build solidarity between both teams and highlight a new type of pattern commensurate with that higher status. But the need for timely reports by Dumitru's engineers was initially rejected by him. He interrupted Cynthia before she finished. For her part, she did an excellent job of providing background details about why the report was needed after these glitches, and it's her work and attention to common ground that made it possible for them to reach a shared understanding. Yet you can see that *full-fledged* was never explained, and Dumitru never got a key reason for the need for the reports. Our recommendation: beware of using idiomatic and metaphorical expressions.

Yet we agree that metaphors add color to otherwise bland speech, and they are ways of expressing ideas in a very compressed form. A Portuguese metaphor suggests that people would rather not be around bland people. A Portuguese speaker might say, to explain a person's nature, that they are *uma pessoa sem sal*—literally, a person without salt (i.e., they're boring). International emails and other communication, though, should be salt free. Metaphors are just not decipherable, and they don't build common ground in these settings. If a Romanian engineer says to you, "I think those guys are just rubbing the mint" (*freacă menta*) or "I'm afraid they're just cutting leaves for the dogs" (*taie frunze la câini*), can you guess what they're getting at? If you're not Romanian, probably not. (Both mean that someone is wasting time.) Or if a Romanian engineer raised a serious question about someone by saying "he's just selling doughnuts" (*a vinde gogoși*), would you guess he means he thinks they might be lying? In Spanish, people with "no hair on their tongue" are not afraid to say what they think. These are interesting expressions, but they create common ground only within a limited cultural group. Otherwise, they disrupt common ground, because their meaning is impossible to guess, even if the literal meaning is well understood. Our recommendation: don't use them.

In one conference call, Mike gave an excellent example of how one *can* use a metaphorical expression in a cross-cultural setting. In his conversation with Rajesh and Arjun, he used a metaphor, but he also explained the metaphor by expressing the idea first and then using the metaphor "bird's eye." He said to Arjun, "Can you give me a look down on it so I can . . . let me take a bird's eye to make sure I got all the information." This is one of the more understandable uses of metaphors we witnessed. Our other recommendation: if you use metaphors, then redundantly add common ground.

Language assumes common ground even without metaphors in those cases when words in one language have no single-word equivalent in another language and must be explained. An example of one such word is the Spanish word *acogojado,* which means "humbly sad." Then there's the Korean *han,* when someone you know makes you feel beat down and alone, and *Torschlusspanik* in German ("gate closing panic"), used when you feel like your life is passing by and opportunities are diminishing. In French, *esprit de l'escalier* ("spirit of the staircase") refers to those times you think of the perfect retort too late. In Hindi and Urdu, *tanha* means a particular type of solitude, a great desire for something with a melancholy feeling. In Finnish *sisu* means having such great persistence toward your goal that no barrier can stop you, a sense of even going through rock if need be. Such words often show up on lists of "words that can't be translated" or "words that English should have," which are misleading headlines: they can be translated, just not in one word. And speakers of any language need those words only if they need to refer to the same common ground. Usually, they don't.

HOW TECHNOLOGY AFFECTS COMMON GROUND

In face-to-face interactions, frames, scripts, and schemas help people understand what activity is going on and what a reasonable person should do next. They function by using environmental and verbal cues, such as how people behave when it's lunchtime or when the boss walks in. In computer-mediated contexts, no matter which colleagues we're talking with and where they live and work, though, we're always in the same onscreen space. There are fewer cues about how different people use frames, scripts, and schemas than there would be if people worked side by side, where there's much more data to observe. When people work in the global office, there are few, if any, opportunities to observe "the other natives," meaning the other people in one's surrounding environment. Technology makes building common ground tougher because there's not much background information visible or hearable. Constantin told us, "We have an open desk [i.e., not a cubicle]. We see each other, we talk to each other. Maybe we communicate with each other more. [But in this global office] we're not getting to know each other, developing friendships, relations, stuff like that." Technology even affects knowing who's there and what kind of scripts, schemas, and frames people are used to.[29]

One of the main ways that computer-mediated communication makes establishing common ground harder is by reducing the number of communication channels that are available. In a face-to-face conversation, people are using a voice channel (if they're hearing) as well as a visual channel (if they're sighted). In a phone call, the visual channel goes away or is limited. Computer-mediated communication reduces the available channels. No matter how good the technology, not all the frequencies of the human voice carry perfectly through the microphones and speakers. Bad connections aren't just annoying; they disrupt the common ground. (And those disruptions, in turn, become opportunities for building further common ground—or losing it.)

"Email English" is famous for generating common-ground mismatches. "I don't allow [my engineers] to send emails without my overview or things can explode," Dumitru told us. Email problems are widespread, as any reader probably already knows. In one study, Australians and Koreans talked about their experiences with international emails. The Koreans saw 40 percent (nearly half!) of incoming emails as lacking politeness, and the Australians thought 27 percent of incoming messages were impolite. Koreans were offended by inaccurate formal titles, and even more offensive was the absence of titles at all. The Koreans said there were not enough face-saving expressions used in many international emails; the messages were too businesslike and didn't open or close properly. The Koreans felt this showed that the sender had no interest in them as a person.[30] Rajesh told us that "it's easy to misunderstand in writing" and "hard to use emotions and feeling." Everyone complained about the rudeness of brief email texts. Email writers missed opportunities to build common ground.

Paying close attention to types of email greeting and how to close an email are simple ways to establish common ground at the beginning of an interaction or communication. Email writers can easily include some language of solidarity, interest, or involvement. Email has a lot of the cross-cultural challenges that successful jokes do. They don't allow for input from the reader/audience, and a lot of assumptions are made about the reader's common ground and prior knowledge. In email, senders often assume that because the technological environment is so similar, the receiver of the email has not only a similar computer screen, but also similar cultural scripts, schemas, and frames. In societies where hierarchy is valued, deferential manners build a common ground of social roles. But in places where hierarchy is actively resisted—for example, in Australia— people are used to different greeting scripts to build common ground.[31] So common ground can be hierarchical or it can be flat, or other variations in between.

When the engineers were looking at the same computer model, and when they went over the designs they had done in model-review sessions, it was easier to build and sustain common ground. Exploring the model together meant that they could more easily understand the way the other was "seeing things." One day Don said to Akhil, "Okay. Now we're in the section with a problem, right? Make sure *we* keep that highlighted." Don's use of *we* created a joint perspective; "make sure" is also a way of directing others to do something that is framed as a reminder (almost like saying, "Perhaps it's not necessary to say this, but . . ."). The same kind of wording can build common ground in emails. An example would be by acknowledging or visualizing the receiver's own world; for example, "*If you have the time,* could you send me a copy." Members of many cultures feel that this not only builds common ground but preserves relationships by giving people a face-saving line of escape if they can't comply right away. It stimulates a ground shared beyond the words of the request (that everyone has limited time).

In our interviews, we asked the engineers what they thought the technological solutions to their communication problems might be. Some of the engineers believed that the best way to build common ground and facilitate the sharing of invisible types of knowledge and invisible assumptions was through more investment in IT and automation to connect colleagues with a kind of knowledge they felt could be packaged and reused. Others thought the answer was a moderate investment in IT but actively facilitating conversations across geographical distance to create an environment where the transfer of tacit or background cultural knowledge was likely to occur. We would vote for the second idea. The main investment ought to be in training people, not investing in better technologies or machines. There's no fixed algorithm for facilitating invisible assumptions and tacit knowledge, but there are some ground rules and heuristics that can be adapted for the global office.

As we mentioned earlier, new capabilities for interaction through computers and email were predicted by pundits to cause enormous changes, such as increasing horizontal contacts within organizations. It was assumed that technology would "undermine hierarchical levels of authority."[32] Hierarchy, however, is an important part of establishing common ground in some cultures.[33] Readers might recognize how this incorrect prediction was based on a lack of common ground—assumptions that people shared common ground in every organization, when they don't.

SOME SOLUTIONS

Everyone has skills for negotiating common ground, as the engineers showed us. Everyone is already multicultural to some degree, since everyone belongs to different groups. For example, technicians have specializations or subfields and use varying levels of formalism. (Thermal engineers use formal knowledge models differently than stress engineers.) This means that everyone is used to tailoring what they say to a "specialized" frame. If you think about it, culture, too, is a form of specialization.

There has been a lot of attention paid recently to the cognitive advantages that bilingual people enjoy, at least on the sorts of tasks that psychologists like to give people. But it turns out that they also have better awareness that their own common ground is only one of several possible modes. They also realize that others have their own behaviors and standards of evaluation (and metaphors). This is what allows them to move between different group standards.[34] Having access to multiple kinds of common ground from different cultures and navigating them successfully is a good way to define multiculturalism.

In the best engineering teams we saw, the engineers actively built and maintained common ground in simple but important ways. They repeated the same thing in different ways. They said what they thought might be obvious (sometimes using politeness terms or a tactful framing such as "Make sure to . . ."). They spoke and heard redundantly. The best team explicitly asked if the other engineers understood, over and over throughout the conference call or meeting. They did this in ways that respected their colleagues' expertise, with utterances like, "You okay with that,

Arjun?" or "Any problems there with that, João?" They also built common ground at the beginning of emails by using a greeting and by sending a few sentences of background linked to the topic. They were careful to close the email with "regards" or a similar phrase. If you can work things out over the phone, that's great, but the communication might be needed in what's the middle of the night to your counterpart. They may be fast asleep because of their time zone, so you might have to write an email. This means it's going to be read probably out of sequence with other emails connected to it, or appear in a different context. It's a good idea to actively provide context so you can have more common ground and more control over others' expectations (like joke tellers have!) and more control over interpretation.

The predictive power of common knowledge about people's behavior is enormous and valuable. Developing common ground is something that has to be actively worked at in the global office. In the following short list are some solutions for enhancing common-ground understandings and managing expectations:

- Different schemas, scripts, and frames are at work in the global office. If you realize that the common ground you thought you had isn't there, treat that moment as part of the job (i.e., as part of the scope of your professional responsibilities). This means you fix the problem by supplying context, expectations, and explanations.

- It's impossible to see people's quizzical or hesitant expressions in a technologically mediated context. If you're sensitive to when an interaction hasn't gone well, or if while it's happening there are uncertainties, say things another way and clarify any references to "it" or "them" or "him" that assumed that your hearer knew the referent and didn't need it specified. Get more material from them, too.

- Continuously supply background information about rationales behind requests and changes in plan.

- For emails, use titles in salutations, if they're expected. Sign off with "Regards" if expected. Doing both shows awareness of the other's common-ground expectations. Make it personal by attending to their familiar scripts.

- Facilitate conversations across geographical distance that go beyond work requests and problems. Create an environment where the transfer of tacit or background cultural knowledge is likely to occur.

- Read a bit about the commonly shared history and culture of those in the global office space with you. Although it's difficult to find time for more things to do, the investment pays off.

- Realize that it takes time to adjust cultural frames. Invest the time. Common ground is built not through rules but through words, and through shared experience.

- Try to avoid any idiomatic or metaphorical speech. When using idioms, duplicate the meaning immediately by saying it another way.

- Be redundant and repetitive. Say the same thing in different ways.

- Continually check for common ground. ("That all make sense to you, Andreea?")

- Understand the role that questions play in each culture, and keep in mind that people frame their uncertainties in varied ways. Actively check understanding at every point.

Building common ground and "matching brains" or "standing in the other's shoes"[35] requires continuous attention, but people are so used to it in their own culture that they don't notice how it's built up over time. Building common ground has to be seen as an important part of the job in the global office. Phrases that show interest and consideration are a way to establish common ground. Email can easily include some language of solidarity, interest, or involvement.

Despite the list we just presented, our goal in this book really isn't to provide a list of do's and don'ts. It's not realistic for people to keep lists of rules in in their heads for use in the global office, where there are many different cultural ideas in play. Rather, our goal has been to provide a deeper understanding of how people make sense of what's going on or what's been said, and the ways culture influences how people talk and understand each other. A focus on underlying action, on the hearer, and on building common ground are principles that everyone can remember to use.

In the next chapter, we delve a bit deeper into culture and explore some noble reasons behind *other* people's exasperating behaviors.

5 Language Is Social (and Cultural)

We're going to spend the first part of this chapter unpacking the following idea: Every utterance contains a theory of the person. Not *who* a person is, but *what* a person is. That's easy, you might say. A person is a person. But what (we'll ask back) *is* a person?

One day, Constantin came into the small office that we used in the Romanian engineering firm. The office was at the end of a long hallway on the second floor, and there were two desks and chairs in it. The office was a great help for us and made it very handy to interview people, and the engineers could find us there when different activities were starting that they knew we wanted to observe, like conference calls and other technologically mediated interactions with the United States. As we chatted with Constantin about his experiences in the engineering company and many other topics, he brought up the topic of email. He suddenly got very serious and intense. He said that when he opened emails from Dave and Don, he often felt like he was not even given the consideration a stranger would be given; he felt they didn't treat him as a person, and he really hated it. "What do they think we are, cattle at the market?" he said.

Over time, we heard many other engineers react to feeling that they were being treated rudely and not being treated as a person. Email seemed to be a major trigger, but other technologically mediated interactions were, too. How could a lack of greeting cause such a strong reaction? We believe it's because every utterance contains a theory of the person—that is, a foundational set of assumptions about what a person is. Constantin's words and the emailed words all contain a theory of the person. Words (and the people who wrote them) caused offense when two (or more) different theories of the person didn't match up. Sometimes there's a corporate or business theory of the person, too, that reflects corporate values and sometimes doesn't match up between companies.[1]

When offense happened, Constantin, Dave, João, and Arjun didn't discuss these experiences as a new theoretical insight into cultural difference. It was rather taken as more evidence for how weird American, Romanian, Brazilian, and Indian ways of life and acting were.

You might have noticed in your travels around the world that you feel treated "badly" at times. You may feel coldly ignored, or discriminated against. And people come home from travels to tell stories about how awful people's behavior was. The models that people use when they're having these experiences and their accounts of how people treated them are ways in which we can see theories of the person at work. When a person doesn't feel treated well in a cross-cultural encounter, it's easy to blame the other person. The problem is that, as observers of human behavior know, people behave out of habit, not logic. So each person, whether they're offending or offended, is simply behaving as they know humans are supposed to behave. But still, people can get terribly offended to the core in cross-cultural situations.

As anyone would, Constantin was using his own theory of a person on the day he reacted to Dave's email and analyzed how badly he'd been treated. Most people use the theory of the person they know, but they also believe that their theory of the person is more than a local one, that it has some worldwide core attributes. So Constantin felt he was entitled to some kind of restitution or at least an apology. How could he get one and get the relationship back on track, though, when Dave thought he had treated Constantin as Dave would want to be treated himself? We'll call this "Constantin's Predicament": a person feels they've been wronged, but they can never get an apology, because the other party can never see that in the first party's eyes they've been offensive.

Unpacking Constantin's Predicament begins by returning to the point we just made: the theory of the person is one aspect of culture that people assume is going to be universal. Therefore, they think apologies are warranted, as Constantin did. What could be more reasonable than the belief that people's biology and physiology leads them to experience the world alike? People don't recognize the enormity of the difference in other groups' theories of the person. Even though, as we started this chapter by positing, theories of the person are in everything we say.

It might be helpful at this point to give a few examples of just how different theories of the person can be. Where is the theory of a person located? We can't find it only by sitting around with philosophers and theologians. In fact, it's right under our eyes. When the Romanians were in the midst of their mania for the television show *Dallas*, they were observing theories of the person being acted out by Texas oil millionaires and other types of persons who, in every line of script, flash of the eyes, toss of the hair, and spurring of the horse, told viewers something about what a person is and how they were supposed to behave.

Even though the modern petroleum engineering office is not half as thrilling or as well costumed as the set of a *Dallas* episode, Constantin's theory of the person and Don and Dave's theory of the person were being performed in every interaction, too. Unfortunately, the players must have felt as if they had wandered onto the wrong Hollywood set, where different scripts and frames were employed (but where they were still reading from scripts they had already memorized, hoping they would still work). Here they flushed from indignation when they sensed an offensive act being done toward them, feeling the hot lights of the theater.

In a similar way, the theory of a person stands out very clearly in media such as magazines and TV. If we go to the local newsstand in the grocery store or the news shop, we see glossy-covered magazines populated with people we'll never meet—a cast of characters, some of whom are ideal persons, some of whom are less than ideal (but more fascinating, let's admit, for how they push the boundaries of moral personhood). Take the ubiquitous "Cosmo quizzes," which *Cosmopolitan* magazine invites its readers to answer in every issue. The magazine analyzes the answers for what they tell you about you as, say, an American person. The quizzes have become part of popular culture, joked about and mocked endlessly. In the magazine the quizzes are somewhat tongue-in-cheek by now. But readers are drawn in by the potential of self-revelation, something new to find out about themselves, their *true* person: "Take this quiz to see what kind of woman is in there (and what's really number one)." "Are you a secret bitch?" "What do you really want?" Other magazines use this format, too, since it's so popular with readers. Magazines like *Men's Health* quiz their readers as well: "Do you have an addictive personality?" "Rate your ability to just say no." "Are you too competitive?" And the Internet site BuzzFeed asks readers to consider: "What city should you actually live in?"; "What Career Should You Actually Have?"; "What Age Are You, Really?"[2]

The questions might at first seem too frivolous to add anything meaningful to a discussion about how the theory of a person varies across cultures. But you probably noticed a lot of the word *you* in the questions. (And writers and editors of these magazines remind the reader "and what could be more important than you!"[3]) You probably noticed that the questions assume that each person is defined by their unique preferences—where to live, what to wear, what objects to buy. It's assumed that for each there's an ideal career path (a kind of personality match, not based on economic need). It seems a bit bizarre when you think about it, but people who create Western Internet quizzes believe that readers have a choice about what age to be (or feel). The theory of the person that lurks behind the quiz holds that a person is a collection of private preferences and choices and takes an individualistic and self-centered path. And if things don't work out, well, there's only one person to blame. You'll never see *Cosmopolitan* put it in such terms. Neither is there much in the quizzes about family influences on decisions or choices, such as how being the eldest child might help determine the right career for you. And when it asks readers the best city to live in, the website doesn't account for where their elderly parents might be or what their religious affiliation is.[4]

In most societies, in fact, a person can make few choices like those described in these Internet quizzes, and choice isn't even thought to be the way to find out who you are. You're born into a network or team, someone's son or auntie, a group that isn't going to function without your help. A single cowboy riding into the sunset preferring the loner's life isn't an option. It might even be considered a sign of mental illness. Preferences are not going to be a guide for predicting future life path or residence, but a close look at family and birth order would be. To make the point: the importance of the family in India is so great, in contrast to other places, that it's sometimes called "familism."[5] The importance of family is pretty widespread, though, but in different ways, across nations—ways different enough to affect theories of the person.

So when engineers are talking about a person, some of them might talk about their own or another engineer's as-yet-untapped individual "potential," but other engineers come from cultures where this kind of self-appraisal is not a very popular pastime.[6] Everyone's culture provides a model of the person that suits most interactions fairly well, but these models don't provide the resources that people need in order to understand, diagnose, and fix cross-cultural mismatches, especially those challenges that engineers in the global office encounter. Different theories of the person aren't recognized until someone feels offended.

How theories of the person are put into action can really go awry in the global office, where many different theories come into contact, as we see in Constantin's Predicament. When we observed engineers, we noticed many times how they could become offended about how they felt they were treated by someone's use of language—an issue to be resolved only with difficulty. They often considered the offense to be intentional. In order to address these breakdowns, we have to focus on what's underneath these feelings of treachery: the theory of the person.

To see how different theories of the person can play out in language and then cause offended feelings, let's step away from the global office into a different kind of global space: international student housing at a university, where offense occurs when ideas of the person clash. The two players are an Indian student and an American one who share living quarters at a U.S. college.[7] After a while, the American roommate starts to complain to her Indian roommate because the roommate's Indian friends keep dropping by at late hours. The American roommate asks her roommate's friends to leave so she can sleep. The Indian student is embarrassed and feels she's been humiliated; she's been raised to believe in a theory of the person that means her responsibilities to her friends are more important than she herself. She tells the American that she should have suppressed her personal, individual dissatisfaction. To the American, this seems as if the Indian student is asking her to repress her true needs and is marking a weakness of character. Precisely the inverse is true for the Indian student: repressing her own needs means she is being strong.[8] (To Indians, to put the self above others hinders their spiritual progress; self-control and sacrifice are praised—like that of a mother toward her children, or a man toward his father—as facilitating spiritual contact with the true inner self.) These two students were both fluent English speakers and had a lot in common. Yet they had very different theories of the person, and each felt highly offended by the other's behavior and justifications. Each felt that she could not "live with" the other person's idea of the person. It's a version of Constantin's Predicament.

The typical interaction on any given day works because the participants share ideas about what a person is. To use a phrase we've talked about before, they have a common-ground understanding. In our observations of engineers, we many times saw them complaining about other engineers because they were unable to shift ground and to understand other engineers' behavior within a different context. Rather, if the person didn't behave as expected, the reaction of an engineer would be to feel frustrated and insulted.

One day Grigore told us about how he had become quite offended when he overheard Jim, a person he felt very friendly with, tell Mike that the American engineers didn't have time to teach the engineers in Romania everything needed for the project. Grigore said hearing this insulted him so much that it inhibited him from asking questions. To him, time spent together and the willingness to spend time signified a good relationship. When people are friendly with each other and are colleagues on the same team, they should always have time to help others. This is a way of saying each person has worth and value. To Americans, time meant value, and Grigore knew that. But what he overheard made him feel worse. He thought Jim's statement that the American engineers "have to teach the [Romanian] engineers from scratch" was pretty insulting. Jim had lumped all into a similar group, a stereotype. In fact, the city where the engineering company was located was the home of the country's top petroleum and gas university, with undergraduate and graduate degree programs. But from Jim's point of view, the cross-cultural collaboration had already taken far more hours than his team had predicted. The project was getting more and more behind, something he was personally responsible for. He didn't think the

Romanian engineers appreciated his situation. What Jim was getting at was the differences in the procedures the two firms used (differences that he felt he had to teach them), not the basic engineering itself. Since the plant they were designing would be built in the United States, those specific codes had to be used.

Even if people were able to train all of their coworkers to expect different theories of the person so that each one understood what drove the other's behavior and incidents of perceived offense to their person, there is the problem of habit. Everyone—including the people who study these processes themselves—finds it nearly impossible to control their behavior, so much of which is habitual. But knowing how local and special a person's own cultural views about the person are (i.e., that they aren't shared among all humans) is a good first step to becoming more flexible and being prepared for offending people and feeling offended. We may have to be vigilant about confirming others' worth, too, to build in resilience.

João may or may not have the right experience with certain English speakers to recognize their theory of the person—that is, one that assumes that the family is "behind" the person's individual achievement (in the background), that individual achievement can even be okay at the expense of the other members of the family, and that those family members expect to gain some prestige from it. Even if he understands this, he may still have trouble activating the theory and acknowledging such behavior. This is the case even though such acknowledgment is necessary for collaboration. His own cultural theory of the person contains the American's model as a *negative* example, so he has trouble not feeling some disdain for Dave and Don's individualistic drives and assumptions. Or maybe Don and Dave have the right experience in Brazil, which enables them to understand that Brazilians work to live and don't live to work. But they still may feel that "live to work" reflects honorable passion for the job and a love of engineering, too. They might also feel some frustration with an attitude that seems not to put the team first. It's hard not to activate negative mirrorings, and negative models about each other, because negative mirrorings are a means of social control through "what not to do" in one's own culture.

The difficulties for all sides become more obvious when people move to another country. Then they find that even within their own family, cracks emerge in the theory of the person and how behavior is seen and judged. As first-generation children grow up in a new culture, the parents realize how different the theories of the person are in the new place. The kids, for their part, feel like "halfies" and talk about the difficult conflicts they have in fulfilling multiple competing ideas of personhood for the family, peers, and the society. There are clashes over what behaviors mean (forms of dress, peer-group activities) and what the family's role is. The kids find comfort hanging out with other halfies. They sometimes adopt an "oppositional youth culture."9 In the more sensational and troubling cases of culture clash, the government gets involved in mediating moral aspects of personhood when ideas of the person are in conflict, such as the autonomy of an individual to make choices versus the family's power over its offspring or the state's rules versus religious ones. All these impinge on or add up to what it means to be a person.

There are no easy schemes or rubrics that can cover all the ideas of a person in the rich variety of human societies. Unfortunately, in order to generalize for all cultures about what people think a person is, the categories of behavior become quite abstract and not so easy to put into practice in an office. One anthropologist studied five subcultures in the United States: the Zuni, Navajo, Mormon, Mexican-American, and Euro-American.10 What he felt best characterized their differences in theories of the person revolved around the following dimensions: whether they considered people to be inherently good or inherently evil or both; people's relationship to the environment; their relationship to time; whether they were expected to fit into a hierarchy or be individualistic; and how the body was thought to have inner versus outer qualities. In another scheme, based on researching corporate life in many different countries, six dimensions of the person were generalized as essential:11 a power distance calculation;12 individualism versus collectivism; uncertainty avoidance, emotion, and gender; long-term versus short-term temporal orientation; and indulgence versus restraint. These schemes tell us something about the level of abstraction needed to account for human diversity (though the concepts often reflect a Western psychological orientation). We lay these out here to show how difficult most of the categories are to apply to a specific case, if we're looking to really appreciate Constantin's Predicament.

Instead of a list of traits, we're going to focus on the idea of "face"—social rejection or social approval. When halfie kids are embarrassed by their parents' idea of how they should behave, when Constantin or Dave feels offended, the concept of "face" can be a good guide to the emotional space of feelings when different theories of the person get acted out. In some cultures, talking about face is omnipresent, but even in cultures where people don't talk about it, face is an important issue in interpersonal relations.

When you're not treated as a person, it means you've lost face.[13] Loss of face often feels like a flush that begins at the base of the neck and seems to travel up to the hair. It's a grim feeling, when the person we think we are gets shown to be something different, something lesser.

What we have been talking about with examples from Grigore, João, Constantin, and the students at the university aren't just theories—they involve real feelings of social embarrassment (rejection) and social approval (acceptance). And we're going to talk about a system of habits or conventions for doing things in every culture both to recognize and approve of a person based on what a person is, and to protect face. A person's sense of self-worth can be threatened by not being seen personally, and by a tendency—one that everyone has—to see another person impersonally as a stereotype, like seeing every American as the same, with the same wants and needs.

If you recall, Constantin's interactions with Don and Dave, and Dave and Don's interactions with Constantin, were full of theories of the person, and they each expected the other to be operating with the same ones—theirs. This explains some of the outrage felt when they didn't get treated well. It also explains why they held the other accountable when the recognition wasn't what they expected.

Earlier we described how Constantin had felt mistreated because emails from Dave didn't come with the expected greeting. To get back to Constantin's complaint about this, we have to talk about how greetings work in theories of the person and how they can be threats to one's face. People can't train their coworkers to analyze theories of the person in every utterance, but they can make sure that the most important rituals of the person are observed (and have culture work in their favor). Although they might seem a trivial part of interacting, greetings are an important ritual in preserving and maintaining face, or recognizing someone's social value.[14] And they're one way in which theories of a person are seen in action.

THE THEORY OF A PERSON IS CONTAINED IN GREETINGS

Dave and Don never said to Constantin, in so many words, "We don't consider you a person." What they did to offend Constantin might seem trivial. After all, they merely failed to use a greeting. And Constantin was left without much way to change this. Could he say, "Please, guys, greet me"? Instead he felt the insult time and again.

It wasn't only Constantin who felt this way. When Bill didn't begin his emails to his Indian counterpart with a salutation, such as "Dear Arjun," or close it with something that signified their connection, like "Regards, Bill," Arjun said, "I feel his arrogance." The absence of a greeting was very disturbing and damaged someone's feelings of worth. To Constantin and others who talked to us, the absence of a personal greeting in an email (such as the simple "Dear Constantin") felt like Dave and Don had reduced them to a nonperson. Constantin's theory of a person included the idea that people were part of a larger family of relationships. When these relationships weren't acknowledged, Constantin felt cut off. Constantin came from a culture where the theory of the person is linked to connections to others. He told us, "You can't only discuss technical problems, you have to discuss other things, family, other issues." Workmates became like a kind of family.[15] To Constantin, his view of himself as a person was not congruent with not being entitled to a greeting. What about all the work they had done together? He felt dumped in a corral, a kind of animal that's never given a name. This not only hurt Constantin, but reflected badly on Dave.

Dave and Don consistently didn't use personal greetings in email. From Dave's point of view, though, he was using a style common in the tech world, where informality (not using "Dear") is friendly, not impersonal. He thought that a lack of greeting showed solidarity that he and Constantin were in the same generation and on the same team. The American engineers left out greetings, they said, because they thought their short, direct emails would be understood as efficient, given there were so few overlapping hours to communicate with one another. But the Brazilian engineers called the American engineers' style "leaving out the human." They said, "The human factor matters more *outside* the U.S."

In greetings, everyone has to acknowledge a type of relationship, sometimes by a quick calculation: Who is this person to me? Who am I to them? In German, this calculation ends by selecting the pronoun *du* for "you" if you have a long acquaintance and explicit permission (or if it's a child), or selecting *Sie* as the more formal term of normal life. In Romanian, Portuguese, and Hindi, too, pronoun choices have to be made when saying something like "How are you?" Maintaining greetings and calling people by name and title recognizes social worth and makes sure that how others see a person's worth remains congruent with how they themselves see it.

When interacting in virtual space and technologically mediated office spaces, there isn't much time or space for showing special regard for others' identity. This doesn't mean email greetings are a "waste of bandwidth," as some IT workers believe.[16] This means "small" and "mundane" things like greetings are even more important. In the technologically mediated office, visibility is a problem. Arjun remarked on the problem of invisibility: "Sometimes it seems like Houston can forget that, you know, there's India in the room. Maybe because there was no visual, they would start talking among themselves sometimes." Forgetting personal greetings exacerbated this feeling of invisibility and lack of importance.

As Arjun's example showed, there are risks of threatening someone's sense of self-worth and face not only in greetings but in ending interactions, too. Ending a conversation too quickly might make the other person feel they have no value or aren't interesting enough to continue to talk to.[17] So in face-to-face conversations or phone calls people have different ways to use words that respect the other. They might, like in the United States, infer that it's the *other* person who doesn't want to carry on talking with them anymore. For example, when Cynthia says to Dumitru "I'd better let you go now," she expects Dumitru to get the real message and to understand that she doesn't want to talk to him anymore because she has other things pressing that she has to do; the call is over. If Dumitru said, "No, no, I don't have to go anywhere," Cynthia would be flustered and might even laugh out of nervousness, and she would be hard-pressed to find something to say. Why don't people just come out and say they want to end a conversation? Why the need for disguising this and creating an elaborate flourish by hinting and then reluctantly going? By saying, "I'd better let *you* go," Cynthia is showing Dumitru's worth by making him the important person. Signing off on an email, like "Regards, Jim," was seen by many of the engineers as a way to end an email that showed recognition of a person and their important role by not abruptly ending. When it was absent, they felt offended. It's important to be vigilant in confirming others and their right to be seen and heard.

MORE ABOUT THE IMPACT OF THEORIES OF THE PERSON

Let's look at another situation illustrating how the theory of the person exists in every utterance, and how unique theories of the person cause predicaments like Constantin's. One day in Brazil, in the beautiful office not far from one of the world's most famous beaches, João and his colleagues began planning a company party to honor some visitors and to build team solidarity, which they felt was lacking. They told us that the other engineers they worked with didn't understand Brazilian culture very well. The party was thought to be a way to reach out and show them some customs of everyday life. The idea fit with notions that Brazilians and many other cultural groups have: that in order to work with people you have to first establish a friendly relationship, which is the basis for trust. American work manuals also talk about the benefits of informal get-togethers to bond and to spread knowledge, but this wasn't taken very seriously by the American engineers. And the technologically mediated office made it difficult, too. João and his Brazilian colleagues eagerly looked forward to an opportunity to develop the deeper friendships and trust that preceded good work outcomes. Especially when relationships are troubled or challenging, it's important to have some informal interactions, too, they felt.

But after everyone had made plans and promises about the party and a schedule had been worked out, something happened. One of the visitors turned out to be the company's HSE (health and safety executive). When he heard about the party, he said it wasn't going to happen. Rio was too risky, too dangerous, and he wouldn't put the American part of the team at risk. The HSE, Jack, invoked his job role to autonomously decide that the local context was unsafe and that a party was potentially harmful to the engineers and staff. In communicating his decision, he used very assertive, bureaucratic language, with rationales about principles of contractual obligations and liabilities. He was very detail oriented and thorough. It was important to him to stick closely to American company policy. His tone, when he told us about the incident, was definitive and sure, not leaving any room for negotiation. There hadn't been any discussion, and he felt he had narrowly averted a disaster.

João and his Brazilian colleagues, though, felt humiliated by Jack's conviction that their city was so unsafe and dangerous that people needed to be under armed guard or behind security fences all the time. After all, Rio was a popular place for tourists (1.5 million foreign tourists in 2011, and increasing every year). That Rio was considered so unsafe that they couldn't even have a company party was insulting. It was as if Brazil weren't a civilized place with civilized people, and as if the Americans could be the judges of this. Brazil has much stronger gun-control laws than the United States, and the United States is the only country in the world that considers owning a gun a right. Brazilians know that Brazil has the most gun murders in the world, but also that the United States has the most gun murders among industrialized nations. The idea that Jack would call Brazil too violent to have a normal work life seemed unfair. The emotional issue of personal justice and the well-known violence of American cities caused indignation. The Americans didn't want to include themselves in normal everyday activities, it seemed.

Jack's attitude about safety was businesslike and impersonal, even indifferent. He didn't understand some of the contradictions in his ruling or show gratitude and appreciation for the efforts of João and his colleagues. People want to be considered likable, competent, hard-working, helpful, and caring about the group. His decision implied that, left to their own devices, João and his Brazilian colleagues would put their colleagues at risk. Jack used threats to safety so that one view could prevail over another. What started out as a way to develop appreciation for another group's worth by finding out how life was lived there ended up providing a stage for the other group to show a lack of appreciation for the others' culture and for the others' competence.

Brazilians in this case weren't seen as competent, righteous, and honorable; they were treated as too fun loving to imagine potential dangers. The implied criticism of those who had fostered the party idea, and the preaching tone of the safety message, divided the teams. The price of ignoring the others' sense of self-worth was high. How could João and the others regain their sense of dignity? In cases of loss of face or threats to face, people often have to resist the urge to counterattack. We heard the Brazilians saying Americans don't want to know anything about them, they think only about getting ahead in the company and avoiding personal responsibility. It seemed to the Brazilians that the Americans' definition of a livable culture did not include Brazil's.

João held his relationship status and autonomy in high regard but was in this case deprived of his value as a relational part of a larger whole. The implication was that he put enjoyment above the safety of the others. He felt that his views on his own culture weren't trusted and respected. For his part, Jack constructed himself as someone with authority over the team, not just at work, but after work. From what João and others told us, we knew that to Brazilians it's important to invest time in getting to know the people you're working with on mutual terms. This is a common way of developing a team. João thought that to Americans, it's not important to develop personal connections. He even felt they preferred not to. Everything Jack did and said confirmed this—and his businesslike style of communication won't go far in many other cultures.

Jack felt he would be individually responsible if anything happened, since he knew that Americans typically looked for the individual responsible, even though the Romanian and Brazilian offices thought more in terms of a team responsibility. Things were more collectively oriented and sanctioned there. (This applied to how praise was distributed, too.) Given his individual orientation, he couldn't see how this scenario had damaged his whole team.

Dumitru also described to us his frustration when people from other cultures didn't show interest in others' ways of being and getting to know them. He asked us:

"Do you know where is the Romania location?" (We did.)

Then he said: "Please make a test. Give Americans a map; give them a test. People cannot understand that in Romania, the civilization is okay, the life conditions are okay, you can find everything in Romania like the U.S. The people are very polite, the food is much better, the coffee is much better. Romania is a very nice country."

Dumitru felt that in spite of his trying to show who he was and create a shared experience as engineers in the global office—through mentioning, for example, all the projects he's worked on with French and Indian customers—the only thing the Americans heard were his occasional problems expressing himself in English (though he speaks three other languages fluently). He said his accent and his Romanian identity prevented others from seeing him as he felt he had every right to be seen. He told Pete and Cynthia during one frustrating conference call: "The information is not reaching you. I have leadership qualities, have had management positions. I like to take initiative."

Most of the time, face is easily maintained when someone keeps their image and their status in line with how their image is reflected back to them by others (in a particular interaction or situation), a kind of image matching.[18] The stage lights go up; all goes well. People in fact help each other (and assume each other's cooperation) in maintaining face in interaction; they do this by essentially not contradicting the image others are putting forward.[19] Sometimes, though, in the global engineering office, because the underlying theories of the person differed, someone's face got pounded. And when their image of who they are as a person wasn't ratified, the engineers didn't just shrug and say "those barbarians" (or ill-mannered people). Rather, they felt a social rupture. In these moments, society becomes to us a kind of mind and body extended from ourselves. And we feel the pain of another's disregard.

One day on a conference call, Constantin was asking Dave once again for some answers to questions that the Romanians had about the engineering design. They still hadn't had an email reply. Dave then said, "I'll get to it when I can." Then Constantin asked for a more specific date. Dave reiterated that he'd get to it when he could. It created an impasse. Different theories of the person and how a person should respond were in play. From Dave's point of view, Constantin should know that Dave was already overworked and what kind of a person he was: he always did his best. (In fact, the Romanian team respected Dave a lot.) Dave relied on his own cultural ideas about autonomy and a need for some autonomy to do the best work. You might say he presented himself as what he thought would be easily recognizable as a person of value—with a need to appear independent, in control, and responsible. For some people and in some cultures, autonomy is linked to preservation of face more strongly than others. But differences in how autonomy is viewed affects whether people believe they are being treated fairly and with personal regard.[20] Constantin didn't feel he was being treated fairly, but rather that he was being left out of any negotiation over delivery times. He felt he had lost face as a person who wasn't negotiated with as an equal.

Here's where we get back to the problem of different theories of the person. In some cultures, individual autonomy is an important part of being an adult, while in other societies it isn't considered that way. (In truth, autonomy is valuable to everyone in some way, even though all societies have to manage it in order to get cooperative stuff done.)[21] The more a society has individuality wrapped up in its theory of a person, the more autonomy will be part of what it means to be seen as a competent person.

One day Constantin was mentioning to us some of the ways that loss of face played out in his work life and caused "emotion." He said he'd noticed that sometimes his design for a support for the structure they were building together with the Americans was "moved from one place to another" without any explanation. He assumed it was because of the different American engineers' own preferences for certain design features, not for any sound structural reasons. But such a change in someone else's design, he said, "involves the emotions and the brain." The emotion included a feeling that his design was slighted in favor of another's autonomous act— and the recognition that nothing was said about it.

Here's another way that the connection of autonomy to theories of the person can lead to predicaments, this time an American predicament. Americans are puzzling to others because they expect to receive a lot of thank-you's. They expect more thank-you's than people from other cultures do in a wider range of instances, and they treat thank-you's as a measure of their worth in the eyes of others. This means they feel a loss of value and face and are offended if they aren't thanked. *Why aren't I being acknowledged?* they ask. Because of how autonomy is part of their theory of the person, acts toward others are not particularly obligatory (not so much as they are in many places). Because of this non-obligatoriness, if not thanked, people become indignant (as Constantin felt without a proper greeting). You might hear them say things like "I have never understood why Indians don't ever bother to thank anyone."[22] Indians for their part think Americans' high volume of thank-you's must mean they don't truly mean anything by saying them.[23]

JUDGING A PERSON BY THE SOUNDS OF THEIR LANGUAGE

Theories of the person are put into action when people hear someone's accent. People establish working theories about a person from just a few accented vowels or consonants. Comedians use this to great effect. The Swedish chef on the TV show *The Muppets* is an example. The puppet didn't actually speak any known Swedish words, but mimicked (in an exaggerated way) Swedish sounds and intonational contours (which Swedes actually thought sounded Norwegian) using nonsense words. The nonsense words sounded foreign and mocked the seriousness of TV cooking shows with exotic ingredients and foreign chefs, and the unexpected mishaps of chemistry in front of a live camera. The comedy sketches typically ended with the equipment or the ingredients—in some cases, a live chicken or goat—getting the better of the chef, something some of us can relate to more than others.

A few sounds are used just like this in every society to mock people based on theories about what an accent "says" about a person.[24] In a U.K. study, those who spoke the "best" English (by which was meant BBC English, not those with regional accents[25]) were also thought to have more positive attributes, such as companionability, than those with regional accents. A theory of the person was based only on their accent, not on any other information about them. Pronunciation in most societies is used this way. Accents are linked to memories of other similar-sounding people[26] (called *indexicality* by sociolinguists and linguistic anthropologists). Theories about a person are triggered by words, such as when people use specialized vocabulary.[27]

Accent is something speakers have little control over and that speakers aren't even aware of having usually. As one Indian writer put it: "When someone tells me I have a slight 'Bengali' accent to my spoken English, my first reaction is to cringe, [then I] insist that I have what I call a 'neutral' Indian accent."[28] What would make him cringe? The type of person he feels people assign to him via his accent, which involves stereotypes he didn't feel fit him.[29] His view of himself was not congruent with what was reflected back to him. This can lead to a kind of Constantin's Predicament, too.

People hear a Swedish accent or a Bengali accent and associate the accent with something not really there, assumptions and theories about what kind of people the speakers are, their background and even beliefs. Hearers make a lot of associations, far beyond what they actually hear even when the words themselves are not understandable, like with the Swedish chef. By asking us if we know where Romania is on a map and by telling us about the superior coffee there (at least compared with the United States), Dumitru is trying to establish some new theories of understanding that go beyond easy theories about him as a person. Establishing new theories enables us to see people differently.

If people don't keep developing new associations over time, certain mappings between the sound of language and what a person is like (e.g., the BBC English accent equaling companionability) come to be perceived, by those who share the same cultural theories of a person, as having some measure of reality. This familiarity makes it easy to forget that the associations are probably wrong.

As you can see, theories of the person can undermine people's efforts to work globally. When you think about how each person is working within their own range of ideas about what a good person is, though, it's easier to handle the feelings of offense and realize that something was lost in translation.

Now we'd like to make two more points related to the theme of this chapter that are important for developing flexible communication skills in the global office. The first point is that what's not said is sometimes as important as what is said. The other point is that what people do say is interpreted against what they didn't say; in other words, a speaker's choice of how to put something into words has meaning by virtue of what hearers know speakers' choices were. Understanding this can make people aware that their intended meaning might not be conveyed completely in what they actually said. And when something goes wrong, it's a signal that their meaning didn't get transferred as they assumed it would.

WHAT'S *NOT* SAID AND WHAT COULD HAVE BEEN SAID

We've mentioned several times how what's *not* said has a lot of social meaning. This is because what's said is always evaluated against what *could* have been said. It's also evaluated on the basis of what might be expected to happen next. Let's take the kind of comments everyone makes at times, the self-deprecating ones. It's been a long day at the office. You do something too quickly and make a mistake, then make a disparaging remark about yourself and your abilities. Your colleagues don't say anything. In this case, the silence of your colleagues is welcome. People generally like agreement,[30] but there are exceptions; they don't want people to agree with them about their failings. So when others don't (openly) agree in this case, they made a choice (in this case, a good one).

In the same way, hearers are always evaluating what someone says against a background of the common choices they know speakers had about what to say. When Pete says to Dumitru, "That drawing just looks weird," the engineers on the conference call knew that wasn't a common choice to describe a professional engineering drawing. Pete's choice indicated that something was very wrong—at least in Pete's perception.

You can look at choices people make about how to say things as analogous to the choices that people have in the way they dress.[31] People make choices to fit the occasion, and what they are wearing gives hints about what kind of frame they're in. An engineer showing up to work in a suit and tie is making a choice in contrast to other choices, such as chinos and a plaid shirt. Fellow engineers will notice the choice and give it meaning. The clothes say something about the role a person will be playing (perhaps going for a job interview), and the role is understood in contrast to other roles that necessitate other costumes. The significance comes through the knowledge that there are different ways to dress. But a person has to choose one, and the one they choose is judged within a range of possibilities available.

The meanings of choices in language can be a lot more subtle than dress. Even when a person is doing something as simple as getting everyone's attention on a conference call, how they choose to do it or what they choose to say (for example, "Let's start") is evaluated partly through what they *didn't* choose. While these background choices are clear to native speakers, they aren't so to many speakers of global English. Let's take a sentence spoken by Pete on a conference call. After a pause in the call, while the engineers were finding some drawings, Pete said: "Okay, gentlemen, back on the wire?" The word *gentlemen* used here was like a suit-and-tie word. It's dressed up. Why would Pete use such a word here instead of *guys*? What might he communicate by this more formal word? The word *gentleman* points to certain social meanings—to a rather old-fashioned, formal context. For one thing, it's the kind of opening that establishes formal roles, like leader and follower. Pete is saying "Let's get started" in a formal way, which gives a heads-up to the hearer that being a hearer will be more formal, too. (And he may be using *gentlemen* in an ironic way, acting in the way that formal people act as a comment on that formality.)

Dumitru answers slowly, "We are, yes, we are still here."

Pete says: "Okay, here's the plan." He starts to explain: "The lateral pipe—"

But Dumitru interrupts: "Wait, wait, no no no, one moment please," and he starts to disagree.

Pete ignores the interruption and continues to give directions. Finally Pete becomes short-tempered with Dumitru's continued input: "Let me finish. Part two is that you're going to take the constant space . . ." He starts to talk slower, emphasizing each word.

In this interaction, the background choices evident in Pete's meeting-restarting phrase "Okay, gentlemen" haven't carried over to the Romanians. The phrase "Okay, gentlemen!" is so well known in American office life that it has spawned a whole cartoon series. The cartoons depict an authoritative boss's message to employees starting with "Okay, gentlemen." In the case of the global office, though, the message meant to be understood—that this is a message from someone who is placing himself as the authority—doesn't work. Pete used it to signal he was about to announce a decision. None of this background is available for the Romanians. Tempers flare because their expectations are not met; they believe the design is still open for discussion, when it's not.

The fact that Pete chose to use *gentlemen* has meaning in contrast to what he *didn't* choose. He didn't say "Okay, guys" or "Okay, fellas" or use other terms with more egalitarian, modern, informal connotations. It's even more noticeable to use *gentlemen* because Americans are known to the other engineers, like the Indians, for their informality (which can be offensive in the case of an American using someone's first name rather than their title and last name).

Here are some other examples of how a speaker's choice is interpreted by hearers within a matrix of potential choices. Take the different ways people might choose to follow up after a job interview by email in Table 2:

Table 2   Emails are about not only what is said but what could have been said

"I feel like the interview went really well, but I'm concerned that I haven't heard anything back in the timeline you promised."	"I just want to check and see if there's any other information you need."	"I'm going on vacation, so this is to inform you that I'm not available in case you email."	(No email sent; interviewee is waiting to hear back.)

Each of these email choices will be interpreted based on the choices people could have made. And these examples all "say" something about the person who wrote them. One emailer would be judged to not understand the importance of hierarchy very well, and to be not very skillful at imagining the boss's point of view or workload. In another emailer's case, the job doesn't seem very important to the sender; vacation takes a priority. The potential employer evaluates these responses in terms of what wasn't said and of memories of what is usually said, and predicts something about how the person might behave on the job. In the engineering offices, what people said (in contrast to what they might have said) was also being used to judge a person's character and predict future behavior.

Working in a global office can be less exasperating if we keep in mind the fact that every culture uses language to build and reflect theories about people and what they do. Underlying everyday language use are cultural theories of the person that can be distinct and unique.

A few notes to close this chapter:

- Each culture has a theory of the person. How this plays out in conversation means that what's seen as respectful to one group might be offensive to another. Understanding underlying theories of the person can help people become more accepting of offenses, especially when feelings are frayed. These cultural notions about the person aren't discardable, because even the smallest of actions and protocols constitute the building blocks of the person; they're connected at the deepest level.

- We judge people unfairly by their accent and the way they sound. While it's impossible to become fully aware of all these meanings, it's a big step to realize the way they work. You could sum it up this way: words have social histories.

- Everything we say is evaluated partly through the choices people know we had about what to say and how to say it. Words and sentences are interpreted as much by what's not there as what is. People make hundreds of split-second choices as they pick their words. Hearers are aware of the choices speakers have. They interpret what speakers *do* say against a background of possible choices.

- Everyone has to pay attention to face and self-image. Unique theories of the person necessitate unique strategies for avoiding feelings of humiliation, embarrassment, or outrage. It's important to reassure people we value them. There are many ways to do this. Greetings and leave-takings are one easy way.

There are no easy schemes or rubrics that can cover all the ideas of a person in the rich variety of human societies. How theories of a person are put into action can go awry in the global office, where many different theories come into contact. These differences in theories usually aren't recognized until someone becomes offended or offends someone. But there is always the possibility of another chance to have a different outcome.

Conclusion

People have enthusiastically taken on new global collaborations with digital technologies to save money, grow opportunity, and to use expertise wherever it exists on the planet. But as Arjun said, if people don't figure out how to communicate better in these contexts, "it will always be like us versus them with a wall in between." The revolutionary technology that now makes it possible to work with colleagues across the globe—email, phones, the Internet—requires good communication skills. Adapting communication to new tools is what humans excel at. Adapting to new cultural environments can also be a source of excellence and innovation.[1]

It's a cliché to say that the world is becoming smaller. But it's also a fact, if you think about how technology has made it possible for widely dispersed people to be part of the same conversation—a fact that has an impact on the working lives of global professionals.[2] You're likely to work with people who don't share your ideas, who speak an accented English with unique phrasing influenced by their first language and culture, who have different ways of doing things with words. If the only interactions that people have take place through digital spaces, it's hard to learn about communication styles by the usual means, like observing what goes on in the office or on the bus. But language still affects getting the job done when there's no shared office.

Executives in many global industries have recognized that differences in communication styles around the world are a thorny problem, and professional engineering societies and educational groups have begun to emphasize "soft skills" training along with training in technical (so-called hard) skills.[3] Engineering work, as one engineer said, "is about the deliverables." The work today includes tracing culture. It includes understanding communication. Most people, like the engineers, don't spend a lot of time discussing what culture is or how communication works. But not taking seriously how people use and understand language can be just as fatal as not understanding technical aspects of the job. As Constantin said, "Almost anyone can be a good engineer, but if he or she cares about communication—then he or she will move ahead."

In this book we have used research findings to build an approach to communicating better in the technologically mediated, culturally diverse global office. We've shown how people in every culture are largely unaware of how much they underestimate background (cultural) information— that is, until something goes wrong. People's use of their own culture to make sense of other people usually is deployed in the background. This leads to a situation, common among the engineers, in which culture is mistakenly seen as just a side issue for global teams until problems develop. What we say and what they say, how we listen and how they listen, even what we expect from communication itself—are all shaped by unique cultural backgrounds. At one level, this is an admirable aspect of humanity. At another level, it easily leads to conflict.

As we have noted, one of the problems the engineers had was that they didn't share the same office. They had little chance to observe each other and informally learn about each other. At first this didn't trouble them: they thought that culture couldn't really matter that much when everyone was speaking English. But they eventually realized that things they thought were universal about engineering were not so universal. Local ways of doing and seeing things became very relevant. When the engineers told us they wanted information about culture, that motivated us to write this book.

As the book has progressed, we have been laying out the details of the Communication Plus model, which is a way of doing communication in the global office in order to make cross-cultural interactions more effective. The story of this model began with recognizing that there's no neutral form of communication and no aspect of communication that's free of culture's influence. As a result, it isn't practical to try to be "direct and clear," since what's clear to a person in one place isn't going to be clear to someone across the world. Being direct can cause offense and can damage the very relationships a person needs to get the job done. It's unrealistic to expect others to adapt to your cultural style of communication, because it's difficult for anyone to be completely aware of how much their own culture influences communication. But in each chapter we've shown key, common principles that underlie all human communication systems and every communication act.

We called our model Communication Plus because we feel that if people add a few key ideas atop what they already know about communication, and change a couple of assumptions, they will be more effective. You as a reader don't have to give up what you do natively, but rather add some principles: start seeing language as action, and start being aware of how you respond to actions. Focus much more on the hearer, build and check common ground actively, and be sure to explicitly acknowledge colleagues' unique human identity.

We believe the only time that the engineers—who were sometimes irritated and exasperated with each other—worked successfully together was when they put into action two ideas. The first idea is that key aspects of cultural *context* are "missing" or unavailable to them because of the technologically mediated settings and lack of face-to-face interaction. We saw engineers (and other communicators) succeed when they recognized this gap and took steps to prevent its negative consequences. The second idea is that all of us are "missing" some cultural *knowledge* in a cross-cultural encounter because of different cultural backgrounds. Engineers (and other communicators) succeeded when they recognized this additional gap and also tried to prevent its consequences. The Communication Plus model is built to provide what's missing, based in large part on what the most successful engineers did.

People working in global offices don't lack sincerity or good intentions. No matter how technically skilled they are, however, people still can't solve their communication problems on their own if they believe that good communication naturally arises out of sincerity or good intentions. This is because everyone has a cultural view of communication that shapes their communicative behavior. However, these influences are invisible to the people using them. In response to questions about culture, people often say, "This is the way we have always done things." The way to become more successful in global office settings is to understand and be aware of your own (invisible to you) expectations about communication (the way you've always done things), which will make you more sensitive to noticing the different expectations of others.

This is important to note because not all cultures have the same ideas and prescriptive advice about how to communicate. Some cultures expect more disclosure from speakers and hearers, for instance, or have different tolerances for ambiguity in conversation. In some cultures it's considered better to be deliberately unclear in order to avoid conflict and to distribute responsibility for outcomes. Good communication in English or any other language is not only a matter of meaning well or getting the grammar right. It's also a matter of knowing how to ensure that the other person feels acknowledged, of expressly getting rich feedback, of paying attention to the hearer's perspective, of seeing the action in every utterance.

Across four cultures, engineers in multiple companies told us similar stories. All of them helped us build the Communication Plus model. There were assumptions about communication that we saw cause trouble among the engineers. Although people might get by with homegrown assumptions when they are working with members of their own culture, these assumptions caused trouble when they were transferred to the global office. They were ways people commonly talk about communication, but they're mostly insufficient for the digital communication environment. These assumptions about communication can damage or limit communications in the global digital office, and we discussed the problems with these assumptions in the introduction. That good communication is direct communication is one of the assumptions that we debunked. Another assumption we showed to be flawed is that the reason for communicating is to transfer knowledge from one person to another. We unpacked the assumption that information is all the same, no matter where it comes from. We discussed problems with the assumption that all hearers can be treated alike. We showed problems with the assumption that if people speak the same language (even if some are not native speakers) they ought to easily understand each other. We also took on the assumption that meaning is always in what is actually said rather than in what's not said, what's hinted at, or what the person is already expected to know. We discussed problems with the assumption that communication is based on a set of clear, rational rules (and that people can tell you what these are). We unpacked the assumption that a good communicator can be described as someone who knows how much information to give. And we discussed the problem with assuming that the effects of culture can be *neutralized* by using the right language or by culture being "checked at the door."

Most of the ways people use language are so habitual that they don't think about it, except when something goes wrong. In this book, our goal has been to bring these habits into awareness and highlight those aspects of communication we found were behind problems we saw. Understanding what's "behind" or what's motivating behavior, we believe, leads to a deeper understanding of communication and how it works in the global office. And deeper understanding means that the concepts can be portable to other situations. Each culture has its own language habits. But with some understanding of the generalities that lie beneath these habits, so to speak, you can generate and build better skills for cross-cultural communication. You can generate compassion for misunderstandings, as well as better control over how to fix things.

Making connections between local settings and global settings is an exciting challenge. Technology has made it essential to pay closer attention to how our culturally based *expectations* and *assumptions* about how others communicate can negatively influence our communication effectiveness. With technology people often lose important background information about other people that they used to be able to depend on for creating good relationships and workable communication.

Different cultural habits in communication—when not recognized— prevent people who are working together on global teams from being successful. Every sentence a person utters or hears is doing something important. But the interpretation of someone else's words is deeply entrenched in cultural habits. With more attention to communication, a cross-cultural work environment can be exhilarating and challenging, with opportunities for new awareness of our own language and culture as well as that of others. We understand others, ironically enough, by first becoming aware of our own behaviors and assumptions about communication.

Rather than try to neutralize culture or pretend that the differences between "us" and "them" are negligible, we built the Communication Plus model specifically with culture in mind. In each chapter we discussed communication principles for the global workplace of the twenty-first century. The principles are broad enough to apply to many cross-cultural situations. The principles of the Communication Plus model as we set them out in the book are as follows:

- *Language is action, not information.* Language is more about getting things done in the world than anything else. Once you realize that language is made up of speech acts and that speaking is about getting things done in the world, you can be sensitive to the fact that your language actions can be misunderstood if those same actions aren't recognizable actions to others of another culture. If what you do with language doesn't look like what someone from another culture does with language in theirs, there will be misunderstandings. What a person says next in conversation can tell you a lot about what action they thought you just did and what they thought just happened. Speakers of languages build up understanding sequentially, through an initiating speech act and a responding one. Because many aspects of communication are routine, people become very good at predicting what might be next in a sequence or what might be upcoming or how something might play out. However, in cross-cultural settings, speakers and hearers can often find their predictions wrong and conversations going in unexpected directions. Be vigilant in monitoring and repairing these sequences.

- *The hearer is the most important player.* In the global, technologically mediated office, the focus has to be on the hearer and getting feedback from hearers. This means training everyone to give and ask for the kind of feedback that's missing from a technologically mediated conversation. This feedback is taken for granted or might be the kind that people express nonverbally in face-to-face interactions. A lot of communication training, especially in corporate environments, is aimed at improving the speaker's behavior. The hearer is often a forgotten participant. In cross-cultural settings that take place through technology or are computer mediated, where many feedback cues are absent, speakers must actively collaborate with hearers on meaning and comprehension. It's also necessary to build accurate ideas about the hearer, their culture, and their communication style. For the naturally curious, this can be an enjoyable part of the job.

- *For people to have successful interactions, they need to build common ground.* Checking if common "ground" has been established or is still there is important in the digitally mediated cross-cultural office. In a cross-cultural interaction, you should assume that less common ground exists than you think, and always provide more. In the best engineering teams we saw, the people were actively and continually building and maintaining common ground in very simple ways. They said what was thought obvious. They were redundant. They were careful not to "oversuppose and undertell," but rather to undersuppose and overtell. They worked with their colleagues' cultural habits about explicitly asking (or not) for clarification. This meant they often asked individual people for feedback on understanding, not the whole group.

- *Language is social (and cultural).* Language use is influenced by and even determined by cultural ideas about what a person is supposed to be. One important way every culture uses language multiple times a day is by recognizing another person's humanity, including their special relationship to an in-group. One culture may show someone's humanity by treating everyone as peers or kindred spirits; another may consider this idea an affront to dignity. When members from each culture interact with such assumptions in operation, they may feel they haven't been treated with humanity. Language can make or break relationships at work. It can also make repairs. Greetings and leave-takings are important rituals for acknowledging human beings. It's risky to leave them out in the interest of short-term speed or efficiency, since the long term is equally important in working relationships.

- *Understand how technology can be a handicap and how to compensate for it.* Technology reduces the signals and cues people are used to depending on for communication. Technology also means a lot of communication is asynchronous, like email. Speakers get few cues from their hearer or reader as they compose what they are writing. Good strategies for working with lost context include providing what might seem like context the person already has. Accommodate for lost context for informal learning by encouraging colleagues to tell you about themselves: find out something about people's experiences, about the geography of the country, the national history, and how history has shaped geography and culture. Learning something about each person's own history also helps to place the way they talk within a background of ideas and relationships. Since requests make up a large proportion of email communication, stay aware of how requests (since they can affect a person's future autonomy and provoke hierarchies) are often made in indirect and ambiguous ways. Increased redundancy and more specific checking of understanding help ensure that technologically mediated interactions work, even though it's true that these communication styles can irritate participants.

Communication Plus is a set of principles that can be learned by anyone and applied in multiple situations. It doesn't require anyone to give up what their own cultural background says is right and wrong about communicating. And its five principles can be learned and put to work immediately. The model is applicable to many settings, not just engineering.

Our goal has been to empower readers with a research-based understanding of how culture influences communication, and how to see culture in communication. This we hope will lead to a better ability to think and react within a multicultural framework. Communication skills based on research are not taught widely enough in schools. But we believe that no matter what a person's background is, they can learn about how culture impacts their communication skills, and put it into practice. Anyone can be a good communicator.

Notes

INTRODUCTION

1. See John Gumperz, *Discourse Strategies* (Cambridge: Cambridge University Press, 1982), for more on intonation misunderstandings cross-culturally.

2. Project Management Institute, "The High Cost of Low Performance: The Essential Role of Communications," accessed November 29, 2015, http://www.pmi.org/~/media/PDF/Business-Solutions/The-High-Cost-Low-Performance-The-Essential-Role-of-Communications.ashx; Project Management Institute, "PMI's Pulse of the Profession: Organizations Waste US$122 Million for Every US$1 Billion Invested due to Poor Project Performance—a 12 Percent Increase over Last Year," accessed November 29, 2015, http://www.pmi.org/Learning/pulse/pulse-communications.aspx.

3. This material is based upon work supported by the National Science Foundation under Grant no. 0729253. Any opinions, findings, conclusions, or recommendations expressed in this material are those of the authors and do not reflect the views of the National Science Foundation.

4. The project principal investigators were John Taylor, Sirkka Jarvenpaa, and Elizabeth Keating.

5. As research by sociologists has also shown; see Harold Garfinkel, *Studies in Ethnomethodology* (Englewood Cliffs, NJ: Prentice-Hall, 1967).

6. Accenture, "Winners in the Digital Economy Will Place People First, Forecasts Accenture Technology Vision 2016," January 26, 2016, accessed March 31,

2016, http://newsroom.accenture.com/article_display.cfm?article_id = 4376 2006.

7. Readers may be interested in critiques of the universality of sincerity and intention. See, for example, Webb Keane, *Signs of Recognition: Powers and Hazards of Representation in an Indonesian Society* (Berkeley: University of California Press, 1997).

8. Igor Kopytoff, *The African Frontier* (Bloomington: Indiana University Press, 1987). See also work on transnationalism, such as C. Bradatan, Adrian Popan, and R. Melton, "Transnationality as a Fluid Social Identity," *Social Identities* (2010): 169–78. See also work by linguistic anthropologists on groups in the United States and elsewhere, such as Norma Mendoza-Denton, *Homegirls: Language and Cultural Practice among Latina Youth Gangs* (Malden, MA: Blackwell, 2008); Angela Reyes, *Language, Identity and Stereotype among Southeast Asian American Youth: The Other Asian* (Mahwah, NJ; London: Lawrence Erlbaum, 2007); Janet Holmes, Meredith Marra, and Bernadette Vine, *Leadership, Discourse and Ethnicity* (New York: Oxford University Press, 2011); Anthony Webster and Leighton Peterson, "Introduction: American Indian Languages in Unexpected Places," *American Indian Culture and Research Journal* 35, no. 2 (2011): 1–18; and Valentina Pagliai and Marcia Farr, eds., "Art and the Expression of Complex Identities: Imagining and Contesting Ethnicity in Performance," special issue, *Pragmatics* 10, no. 1 (March 2000).

9. E. E. Evans-Pritchard, *Witchcraft, Oracles and Magic among the Azande* (Oxford: Oxford University Press, 1937), cites an example from North Central Africa of a granary that collapsed. The falling structure injured the people sitting under it. The people explained this event in both empirical terms (i.e., that termites had eaten the supports) and also in terms of witchcraft to make sense of why particular individuals were sitting at that place at the moment the building failed.

10. Sirkka L. Jarvenpaa and Dorothy Leidner, "Communication and Trust in Global Virtual Teams," *Organization Science* 10, no. 6 (1999): 791–815.

11. See, for example, Deborah Tannen, *Talking from 9 to 5: How Women's and Men's Conversational Styles Affect Who Gets Heard, Who Gets Credit, and What Gets Done at Work* (New York: William Morrow, 1994); and Deborah Cameron, *The Myth of Mars and Venus: Do Men and Women Really Speak Different Languages?* (Oxford: Oxford University Press, 2007).

12. John Austin, *How to Do Things with Words* (Oxford: Clarendon Press, 1962).

13. See, for example, Emmanuel Schegloff and Gail Jefferson, "A Simplest Systematics for the Organization of Turn-Taking for Conversation," *Language* 50 (1974): 696–735.

14. But see Don Brenneis, "Shared Territory: Audience, Indirection and Meaning," *Text* 6, no. 3 (1986): 339–47; and Charles Goodwin and Marjorie

Goodwin, "Concurrent Operations on Talk: Notes on the Interactive Organization of Assessments," *IPrA Papers in Pragmatics* 1 no. 1 (1987): 1–55.

15. For more on common ground see, for example, Herbert Clark, *Using Language* (New York: Cambridge University Press, 1996).

16. Harvey Sacks and E. A. Schegloff, "Two Preferences in the Organization of Reference to Persons in Conversation and Their Interaction," in *Everyday Language: Studies in Ethnomethodology*, ed. G. Psathas (New York: Irvington Press, 1979), 15–21.

17. See Alessandro Duranti, *Introduction to Linguistic Anthropology* (New York: Cambridge University Press, 1997); William F. Hanks, *Language and Communicative Practice* (Boulder, CO: Westview Press, 1996); Laura Ahearn, *Living Language* (Malden, MA: Wiley-Blackwell, 2012); Leila Monaghan, Jane E. Goodman, and Jennifer Meta Robinson, *A Cultural Approach to Interpersonal Communication* (Malden, MA: Wiley-Blackwell, 2012); Per Linell, *Approaching Dialogue: Talk, Interaction and Contexts in Dialogical Perspectives* (Amsterdam: John Benjamins, 1998); Teun van Dijk, *Discourse and Power* (Houndsmills, UK: Palgrave-Macmillan, 2008); and Elizabeth Keating and Maria Egbert, "Conversation as a Cultural Activity," in *A Companion to Linguistic Anthropology*, ed. A. Duranti (Malden, MA: Blackwell, 2004), 169–96.

18. See Alice Marwick and Danah Boyd, "'I Tweet Honestly, I Tweet Passionately': Twitter Users, Context Collapse, and the Imagined Audience," *New Media and Society* 13 (2011): 96–113. Also see Jannis Androutsopoulos, "Languaging When Contexts Collapse: Audience Design in Social Networking," *Discourse, Context and Media* 4–5 (2014): 62–73; and Ilana Gershon, *The Break-Up 2.0: Disconnecting over New Media* (Ithaca, NY: Cornell University Press, 2010).

1. COMMUNICATION IN THE WILD

1. For more on context, see Alessandro Duranti and Charles Goodwin, *Rethinking Context: Language as an Interactive Phenomenon* (New York: Cambridge University Press, 1992); and Peter Auer, "Context and Contextualization," in *Key Notions for Pragmatics*, ed. Jef Verschueren and Jan-Ola Östman (Philadelphia: John Benjamins, 2009), 86–101.

2. Language in one conversation influences other conversations as people extrapolate, "decontextualize," and extract prototypical examples or experiences from one context or community and then "recontextualize" these relationships. See Richard Bauman and Charles L. Briggs, *Voices of Modernity: Language Ideologies and the Politics of Inequality* (New York: Cambridge University Press, 2003).

3. For an interesting example of such problems in intercultural translation, see I. M. García Sánchez, M. F. Orellana, and M. Hopkins, "Facilitating Intercultural

Communication in Parent-Teacher Conferences: Lessons from Child Translators," *Multicultural Perspectives* 13, no. 3 (2011): 148–54. For a discussion of the difficulties businesspeople face in adapting to cross-cultural differences, see Catherine Cramton and Pamela Hinds, "An Embedded Model of Cultural Adaptation in Global Teams," *Organization Science* 25, no. 4 (July/August 2014): 1056–81. For an interesting discussion of cross-cultural negotiation, see Richard H. Solomon and Nigel Quinney, *American Negotiating Behavior* (Washington, DC: USIP Press, 2010).

4. For more details on ways to communicate respect, see, for example, Asif Agha, *Language and Social Relations* (New York: Cambridge University Press, 2007).

5. See M.J. Reddy, "The Conduit Metaphor: A Case of Frame Conflict in Our Language about Language," in *Metaphor and Thought,* ed. A. Ortony (Cambridge: Cambridge University Press, 1979), pp. 284–310.

6. Haru Yamada and Deborah Tannen, *Different Games, Different Rules: Why Americans and Japanese Misunderstand Each Other* (New York: Oxford University Press, 1997).

7. For how nonnative English speakers can feel status loss in global English settings, see T. Neeley, "Language Matters: Status Loss and Achieved Status Distinctions in Global Organizations," *Organization Science* 24, no. 2 (2013): 476–97. For examples of language ideology, see Alexandra Jaffee, "Discourses of Endangerment: Contexts and Consequences of Essentializing Discourses," in *Discourses of Endangerment: Interests and Ideology in the Defense of Languages,* ed. Alexandre Duchene and Monica Heller (London: Continuum, 2007), 57–75. Also see Keith Walters and Michal Brody, eds., *What's Language Got to Do with It?* (New York: W.W. Norton, 2005). On language purity, see Deborah Cameron, *Verbal Hygiene* (New York: Routledge, 1995).

8. Jack Lynch, *The Lexicographer's Dilemma* (New York: Bloomsbury, 2009), 15–16. See also Marcyliena H. Morgan, *Language, Discourse and Power in African American Culture* (New York: Cambridge University Press, 2002).

9. For more on these complex relationships, see Joseph Errington, *Linguistics in a Colonial World: A Story of Language, Meaning, and Power* (Malden, MA: Blackwell, 2008); and Bambi Schieffelin, Kathryn Woolard, and Paul Kroskrity, eds., *Language Ideologies: Practice and Theory* (New York: Oxford University Press, 1998).

10. Braj B. Kachru, "Models of English for the Third World: Whiteman's Linguistic Burden or Language Pragmatics?" *TESOL Quarterly* 10 (1976): 221–39.

11. For more on this, see Jenny Cheshire, ed., *English around the World: Sociolinguistic Perspectives* (Cambridge: Cambridge University Press, 1991); A. Pennycook, *Global Englishes and Transcultural Flows* (New York: Routledge, 2007); and H. Samy Alim, Awad Ibrahim, and Alastair Pennycook, *Global Linguistic*

Flows: Hip Hop Cultures, Youth Identities, and the Politics of Language (New York: Routledge, 2009).

12. For more about global English, see Jan Blommaert, *The Sociolinguistics of Globalization* (Cambridge: Cambridge University Press, 2010). For more about nonnative speaker issues, see Betsy Rymes, "Communicative Repertoires and English Language Learners," in *The Education of English Language Learners: Research to Practice*, ed. M. Shatz and L. C. Wilkinson (New York: Guilford Press, 2010).

13. S. Krishna, S. Sahay, and G. Walsham, "Managing Cross-Cultural Issues in Global Software Outsourcing," *Communications of ACM* 47 (2004): 62–66, looks at some implications for particular societies' distinct ways of working, and how these ways can prove problematic when cross-border collaboration is attempted.

14. See Don Brenneis, "Approaches to the Study of Gossip," in *Folklore, Cultural Performances, and Popular Entertainments: A Communications-Centered Handbook*, ed. Richard Bauman (Oxford: Oxford University Press, 1992), 150–53; and Niko Besnier, *Gossip and the Everyday Production of Politics* (Honolulu: University of Hawaii Press, 2009).

15. This is a principle discussed by conversation analysts.

16. Henny Penny is the main character in a folk tale about a chicken who believes the world is coming to an end. The phrase "The sky is falling!" features prominently in the story, and has passed into the English language as a common idiom indicating a hysterical or mistaken belief that disaster is imminent. The boy who cried wolf got attention for warning people, but there was no danger, so people didn't believe him when danger really appeared.

17. See Michele J. Gelfand, Miriam Erez, and Zeynep Aycan, "Cross-Cultural Organizational Behavior," *Annual Review of Psychology* 58 (2004): 479–514, for how cultural differences in organizational behavior can take various forms, and how many efforts to explain cultural differences are still too narrowly focused on individualism-collectivism to explain variance in organizational behavior across cultures.

18. For more on culture from an anthropologist's standpoint, see Alessandro Duranti, *Introduction to Linguistic Anthropology* (Cambridge: Cambridge University Press, 1997). See also Paul Garrett, "Language Socialization and the (Re) Production of Bilingual Subjectivities," in *Bilingualism: A Social Approach*, ed. Monica Heller (New York: Palgrave Macmillan, 2007), 233–56; and Greg Urban, *Metaculture: How Culture Moves through the World* (Minneapolis: University of Minnesota Press, 2001).

19. Alfred L. Kroeber and Clyde Kluckhohn, *Culture: A Critical Review of Concepts and Definitions*, Papers 47, no. 1 (Cambridge, MA: Peabody Museum of Archaeology and Ethnology, 1952).

20. R. M. Krauss and S. R. Fussell, "Perspective-Taking in Communication: Representations of Others' Knowledge in Reference," *Social Cognition* 9 (1991): 2–24.

21. See, for example, Emmanuel Schegloff, *Sequence Organization in Interaction: A Primer in Conversation Analysis*, vol. 1 (Cambridge: Cambridge University Press, 2007); and Paul Drew and John Heritage, *Talk at Work: Interaction in Institutional Settings* (Cambridge: Cambridge University Press, 1993).

22. Godfrey Lienhardt, *Divinity and Experience: The Religion of the Dinka* (Oxford: Oxford University Press, 1961).

23. Constance Classen, David Howes, and Anthony Synnott, *Aroma: The Cultural History of Smell* (New York: Routledge, 1994), 114.

24. Bronislaw Malinowski and Havelock Ellis, *The Sexual Life of Savages in North-Western Melanesia: An Ethnographic Account of Courtship, Marriage, and Family Life among the Natives of the Trobriand Islands, British New Guinea* (New York: Horace Liveright, 1929), page 44.

25. For more discussion, see Michel Kefer and Johan van der Auwera, *Meaning and Grammar: Cross-Linguistic Perspectives* (Berlin and New York: Mouton de Gruyter, 1992).

26. For those with doubts, see John McWhorter, *The Language Hoax: Why the World Looks the Same in Any Language* (New York: Oxford University Press, 2014); for those who see correlations, see John Lucy, *Language Diversity and Thought: A Reformulation of the Linguistic Relativity Hypothesis* (New York: Cambridge University Press, 1992). Also see Asifa Majid, Melissa Bowerman, Sotaro Kita, Daniel B. M. Haun, and Stephen C. Levinson, "Can Language Restructure Cognition? The Case for Space," *Trends in Cognitive Sciences* 8, no. 3 (March 2004): 108–14.

27. See, for example, Peter Redfield, *Space in the Tropics: From Convicts to Rockets in French Guiana* (Berkeley: University of California Press, 2000); and Elizabeth Keating, "Space and Its Role in Social Stratification in Pohnpei, Micronesia," in *Representing Space in Oceania: Culture in Language and Mind*, ed. Giovanni Bennardo (Canberra: Pacific Linguistics, 2002), 201–13.

28. See G. S. Aikenhead and O. Jegede, "Cross-Cultural Science Education: A Cognitive Explanation of a Cultural Phenomenon," *Journal of Research in Science Teaching* 36, no. 3 (1999): 269–87.

29. For more about slang in Rio de Janeiro and some political and social links, see Jennifer Roth-Gordon, "The Language That Came Down the Hill: Slang, Crime, and Citizenship in Rio de Janeiro," *American Anthropologist* 111, no. 1 (2009): 57–68.

30. R. Scarcella and R. Brunak, "On Speaking Politely in a Second Language," *International Journal of the Sociology of Language* 27 (1981): 59–75.

31. *Next action* is a term used in conversation analysis; see Emanuel A. Schegloff, *Sequence Organization in Interaction* (Cambridge: Cambridge University Press, 2007).

32. R. E. Kraut, S. H. Lewis, and L. W. Swezey, "Listener Responsiveness and the Coordination of Conversation." *Journal of Personality and Social Psychology* 43 (1982): 718–31.

33. For a discussion of attempts to encourage such informal encounters, see Anne-Laure Fayard and John Weeks, "Who Moved My Cube?" *Harvard Business Review* 89, nos. 7/8 (July/August 2011): 102–10.

2. LANGUAGE IS ACTION

1. The epic poem *Beowulf* (with its origins in Scandinavia), the oldest known long poem in English, describes scenes like this in some of its 3,182 lines (though the verbal action takes place in beer halls, not the forest).

2. See John Austin, *How to Do Things with Words* (Oxford: Clarendon Press, 1962).

3. John Searle and Daniel Vanderveken, *Foundations of Illocutionary Logic* (New York: Cambridge University Press, 1985); Robert M. Krauss and Chi-Yue Chiu, "Language and Social Behavior," in *Handbook of Social Psychology*, ed. S. T. Fiske, D. T. Gilbert, and G. Lindsey (Boston: McGraw-Hill, 1998), 2:41–88.

4. Stephen C. Levinson quoted in Paul Drew, "Turn Design," in *The Handbook of Conversation Analysis*, ed. Jack Sidnell and Tanya Stivers (Malden, MA: Wiley-Blackwell, 2013), 140.

5. Emanuel A. Schegloff, *Sequence Organization in Interaction* (Cambridge: Cambridge University Press, 2007).

6. Tanya Stivers, Nick J. Enfield, Penelope Brown, C. Englert, M. Hayashi, Trina Heinemann, and Stephen Levinson, "Universals and Cultural Variation in Turn-Taking in Conversation," *Proceedings of the National Academy of Sciences* 106, no. 26 (2009): 10587–92.

7. John Heritage, "Designing Questions and Setting Agendas in the News Interview," in *Studies in Language and Social Interaction*, ed. Philip Glenn, Curtis Lebaron, and Jenny Mandelbaum (Mahwah, NJ: Erlbaum, 2002), 57–90.

8. Stephen C. Levinson, *Pragmatics* (Cambridge: Cambridge University Press, 1983).

9. F. Baird, C. Moore, and A. Jagodzinski, "An Ethnographic Study of Engineering Design Teams at Rolls-Royce Aerospace," *Design Studies* 21, no. 4 (2000): 333–55.

10. Harold Garfinkel, *Studies in Ethnomethodology* (Englewood Cliffs, NJ: Prentice-Hall, 1967), 48.

11. For a study looking at the codification of knowledge and its effect on coordination, see J. Kotlarsky, H. Scarbrough, and I. Oshri, "Coordinating Expertise

across Knowledge Boundaries in Offshore-Outsourcing Projects: The Role of Codification," *MIS Quarterly* 38, no. 2 (2014): 607–28.

12. Wayne F. Hill and Cynthia J. Öttchen, *Shakespeare's Insults* (New York: Three Rivers Press, 1995).

13. Jonathan Culpeper, "Impoliteness: Using Language to Cause Offence: Full Research Report," in *ESRC End of Award Report*, RES-063-27-0015 (Swindon, UK: ESRC, 2009).

14. See Christian Heath and Paul Luff, "Disembodied Conduct: Interactional Asymmetries in Video-Mediated Communication," in *Technology in Working Order*, ed. G. Button (London: Routledge, 1993), 35–54, for combining types of interactional spaces. See Hyo-Joo Han, Starr Roxanne Hiltz, Jerry Fjermestad, and Yuanqiong Wang, "Does Medium Matter? A Comparison of Initial Meeting Modes for Virtual Teams for an Experimental Setting Using Different Types of Media on Projects," *IEEE Transactions on Professional Communication* 54, no. 4 (November 2011): 376–91; and on technology and communication repertoires, see Mary Beth Watson-Manheim and France Bélanger, "Communication Media Repertoires: Dealing with the Multiplicity of Media Choices," *MIS Quarterly* 31, no. 2 (June 2007): 267–93. See Juliana Sutanto, Atreyi Kankanhalli, and Bernard Tan, "Deriving IT-Mediated Task Coordination Portfolios for Global Virtual Teams," *IEEE Transactions on Professional Communication* 54, no. 2 (June 2011): 133–51, for discussions of multiple media at work.

15. I. Arminen and A. Weilenmann, "Mobile Presence and Intimacy: Reshaping Social Actions in Mobile Contextual Configuration," *Journal of Pragmatics* 41, no. 10 (2009): 1905–23. For a study on relationships between communication and temporal boundaries, see J.N. Cummings, J.A. Espinosa, and C.K. Pickering, "Crossing Spatial and Temporal Boundaries in Globally Distributed Projects: A Relational Model of Coordination Delay," *Information Systems Research* 20, no. 3 (2009): 420–39.

16. For research on adapting to technology, see Pernille Bjørn and Ojelanki Ngwenyama, "Technology Alignment: A New Area in Virtual Team Research," *IEEE Transactions on Professional Communication* 53, no. 4 (December 2010): 382–400; and Petra M. Bosch-Sijtsema and Anu Sivunen, "Professional Virtual Worlds Supporting Computer-Mediated Communication, Collaboration, and Learning in Geographically Distributed Contexts," *IEEE Transactions on Professional Communication* 56, no. 2 (June 2013): 160–75. For work on the potential of virtual workspaces, see Arvind Malhotra and Anne Majchrzak, "Virtual Workspace Technologies," *MIT Sloan Management Review* 46, no. 2 (Winter 2005): 11–14. For work on the importance of managing conflict, see Mitzi M. Montoya-Weiss, Anne P. Massey, and Michael Song, "Getting It Together: Temporal Coordination and Conflict Management in Global Virtual Teams," *Academy of Management Journal* 44, no. 6 (December 2001): 1251–62.

3. THE HEARER

1. R. Stephens and C. Umland, "Swearing as a Response to Pain Effect of Daily Swearing Frequency," *Journal of Pain* 12, no. 12 (December 2011): 1274–81.

2. Steven Pinker, *The Stuff of Thought: Language as a Window into Human Nature* (New York: Viking, 2007).

3. E. Rassin and P. Muris, "Why Do Women Swear? An Exploration of Reasons for and Perceived Efficacy of Swearing in Dutch Female Students," *Personality and Individual Differences* 38 (2005): 1669–74.

4. On the importance of communicative responses, see J. L. Gibbs, "Dialectics in a Global Software Team: Negotiating Tensions across Time, Space and Culture," *Human Relations* 62 (2009): 905–35. On the importance of the hearer, see Anna Livia and Kira Hall, "'It's a Girl': Bringing Performativity Back to Linguistics," in *Queerly Phrased: Language, Gender, and Sexuality*, ed. Anna Livia and Kira Hall (New York: Oxford University Press, 1997), 3–18.

5. But see Alessandro Duranti, "The Audience as Co-author: An Introduction," *Text—Interdisciplinary Journal for the Study of Discourse* 6, no. 3 (2009): 239–48; and Charles Goodwin and Marjorie Goodwin, "Assessments and the Construction of Context," in *Rethinking Context: Language as an Interactive Phenomenon*, ed. Alessandro Duranti and Charles Goodwin (Cambridge: Cambridge University Press, 1992), 147–90.

6. On impacts of physical distance on understanding in teams, see Jeanne Wilson, Brad Crisp, and Mark Mortensen, "Extending Construal-Level Theory to Distributed Groups: Understanding the Effects of Virtuality," *Organization Science* 24, no. 2 (March/April 2013): 629–44.

7. See, for example, H. P. Grice, *Studies in the Way of Words* (Cambridge, MA: Harvard University Press, 1989).

8. Hans-Georg Gadamer, *Truth and Method* (New York: Crossroad, 1989).

9. This phenomenon, together with keeping the hearer in mind when you speak, is called *recipient design* by conversation analysts.

10. Norman Miller, Geoffrey Maruyama, Rex Beaber, and Keith Valone, "Speed of Speech and Persuasion," *Journal of Personality and Social Psychology* 34, no. 4 (October 1976): 615–24.

11. R. M. Krauss, W. Apple, N. Morency, C. Wenzel, and W. Winton, "Verbal, Vocal, and Visible Factors in Judgments of Another's Affect," *Journal of Personality and Social Psychology* 40 (1981): 312–20.

12. Claudia Tate, *Black Women Writers at Work* (New York: Continuum, 1983), 92.

13. Elinor Ochs, *Culture and Language Development: Language Acquisition and Language Socialization in a Samoan Village* (Cambridge: Cambridge University Press, 1988).

14. See Ludwig Wittgenstein, *Philosophical Investigations* (Oxford: Blackwell, 2001).

15. For a view of tensions in global teams, see Pamela J. Hinds, Tsedal B. Neeley, and Catherine Durnell Cramton, "Language as a Lightning Rod: Power Contests, Emotion Regulation, and Subgroup Dynamics in Global Teams," *Journal of International Business Studies* 45 (2014): 536–61; and N. Levina and E. Vaast, "Innovating or Doing as Told? Status Differences and Overlapping Boundaries in Offshore Collaboration," *MIS Quarterly* 32, no. 2 (2008): 307–32.

16. On team members' isolation and identification with other team members, see Michael Boyer O'Leary and Mark Mortensen, "Go (Con)figure: Subgroups, Imbalance, and Isolates in Geographically Dispersed Teams," *Organization Science* 21, no. 1 (January/February 2010): 115–31; and J.T. Polzer, C.B. Crisp, S.L. Jarvenpaa, and J.W. Kim, "Extending the Faultline Model to Geographically Dispersed Teams: How Collocated Subgroups Can Impair Group Functioning," *Academy of Management Journal* 49, no. 4 (2006): 679–92.

17. Marina Jirotka, Nigel Gilbert, and Paul Luff, "On the Social Organisation of Organisations," *Computer Supported Cooperative Work* 1, nos. 1–2 (1992): 95–118.

18. For more on relationships between language, ideology, and identity in the case of European identity, see Susan Gal and Judith Irvine, "The Boundaries of Languages and Disciplines: How Ideologies Construct Difference," *Social Research* 62, no. 4 (Winter 1995): 967.

19. Denise Roman, *Fragmented Identities: Popular Culture, Sex, and Everyday Life in Postcommunist Romania* (Lanham, MD: Lexington Books/Rowman & Littlefield, 2003).

20. Janet F. Werker and R.C. Tees, "Cross-Language Speech Perception: Evidence for Perceptual Reorganization during the First Year of Life," *Infant Behavior and Development* 7 (1984): 49–63.

21. Hiromu Goto, "Auditory Perception by Normal Japanese Adults of the Sounds 'l' and 'r,'" *Neuropsychologia* 9, no. 3 (1971): 317–23.

22. A homophone is a word that is pronounced the same as another word but has a different meaning, and could have a different spelling, like *two* and *too*.

23. *Huffington Post*, December 9, 2013.

24. Clyde Kluckhohn, *Mirror for Man* (New York: Fawcett, 1949), 11.

25. J.-L. Chae, H.L. Lim, and M.H. Fisher, "Teaching Mathematics at the College Level: International TAs' Transitional Experiences," *PRIMUS* 19, no. 3 (2009): 245–59.

26. J.W. McGuire, "Personality and Attitude Change: An Information-Processing Theory," in *Psychological Foundations of Attitudes*, ed. A.G. Greenwald, T.C. Brock, and T.M. Ostrom (New York: Academic Press, 1968), 171–96.

27. G. Hofstede, "Motivation, Leadership, and Organization: Do American Theories Apply Abroad?" *Organizational Dynamics* 9 no. 1 (Summer 1980): 42–63.

28. L. S. Vygotsky, *Thinking and Speech* (New York: Plenum, 1987).

29. G. Hofstede, "The Role of Cultural Values in Economic Development," in *Economics and Values*, ed. L. Arvedson, I. Hägg, M. Lönnroth and B. Rydén (Stockholm: Almqvist & Wiksell International, 1986), 122–35.

30. Carolyn Edwards, cited in Barbara Rogoff, *The Cultural Nature of Human Development* (New York: Oxford University Press, 2003), 6.

31. J. Rabain-Jamin, "Language and Socialization of the Child in African Families Living in France," in *Cross-Cultural Roots of Minority Child Development*, ed. P. M. Greenfield and R. R. Cocking (Hillsdale, NJ: Erlbaum, 1994), 150–69.

32. See examples in H. H. Clark, "Responding to Indirect Speech Acts," *Cognitive Psychology* 11 (1979): 430–77.

33. See, for example, N. Bell and S. Attardo, "Failed Humor: Issues in Nonnative Speakers' Appreciation and Understanding of Humor," *Intercultural Pragmatics* 7, no. 3 (2010): 423–47.

34. See, for example, Makoto Hayashi, Geoffrey Raymond, and Jack Sidnell, *Conversational Repair and Human Understanding* (Cambridge: Cambridge University Press, 2013); and Joanne Meredith and Elizabeth Stokoe, "Repair: Comparing Facebook 'Chat' with Spoken Interaction," *Discourse & Communication* 8, no. 2 (2014): 181–207.

4. HOW TO MAKE THEIR JOKES FUNNY

1. This joke was retold by a student in Elizabeth's undergraduate glass in culture and communication. For more on Nigerian jokes, proverbs, and so forth, see Emmanuel Taiwo Babalola and Paul Ayodele Onanuga, "Atrophization of Minority Languages: Indigenous Folktales to the Rescue," *International Journal of Linguistics* 4, no. 1 (2012).

2. Herbert H. Clark and Edward F. Schaefer, "Contributing to Discourse," *Cognitive Science* 13 (1989): 259–94.

3. See P. J. Hinds and C. D. Cramton, "Situated Coworker Familiarity: How Site Visits Transform Relationships among Distributed Workers," *Organization Science* 25, no. 3 (2014): 794–814, on the idea of situated familiarity.

4. F. Trompenaars, *Riding the Waves of Culture* (London: Economist Books, 1993).

5. See also Catherine Durnell Cramton, "The Mutual Knowledge Problem and Its Consequences for Dispersed Collaboration," *Organization Science* 12, no. 3, (May/June 2001): 346–71.

6. Michael Polyani, *The Tacit Dimension* (London: Routledge, 1966).

7. For a discussion about how documents, graphs and other items containing information can be perceived and used differently by different people but

can facilitate knowledge representation even in virtual settings, see P. Alin, J. Iorio, and J. E. Taylor, "Digital Boundary Objects as Negotiation Facilitators: Spanning Boundaries in Virtual Engineering Project Networks," *Project Management Journal* 44, no. 3 (2013): 48–63; and M. K. Di Marco, P. Alin, and J. E. Taylor, "Exploring Negotiation through Boundary Objects in Global Design Project Networks," *Project Management Journal* 43, no. 3 (2012): 24–39. There are relationships between written documents, material substances, and knowledge that must be learned; see P. Luff, C. Heath, H. Kuzuoka, J. Hindmarsh, K. Yamazaki, and S. Oyama "Fractured Ecologies: Creating Environments for Collaboration," *Human-Computer Interaction* 18, nos. 1/2 (March 2003): 51–84.

8. Pierre Bourdieu, *Outline of a Theory of Practice* (Cambridge: Cambridge University Press, 1977).

9. See P. M. Leonardi and D. E. Bailey, "Transformational Technologies and the Creation of New Work Practices: Making Implicit Knowledge Explicit in Task-Based Offshoring," *MIS Quarterly* 32, no. 2 (2008): 159–76, for a list of practices found useful in another study of engineers.

10. See, for example, Rodger C. Schank and Robert P. Abelson, *Scripts, Plans, Goals and Understanding* (Hillsdale, NJ: Erlbaum, 1977).

11. F. C. Bartlett, *Remembering: A Study in Experimental and Social Psychology* (Cambridge: Cambridge University Press, 1932).

12. There is also a nice account of the role of culture in interpreting stories in Laura Bohannon, "Shakespeare in the Bush," *Natural History,* August–September 1966, http://www.naturalhistorymag.com/picks-from-the-past/12476/shakespeare-in-the-bush.

13. W. F. Brewer, and J. C. Treyens, "Role of Schemata in Memory for Places," *Cognitive Psychology* 13 (1981): 207–30.

14. Rodger C. Schank and Robert P. Abelson, *Scripts, Plans, Goals and Understanding* (Hillsdale, NJ: Erlbaum, 1977).

15. See Gregory Bateson, *Steps to an Ecology of Mind* (Chicago: University of Chicago Press, 1972); and Marvin Minsky, "A Framework for Representing Knowledge," in The Psychology of Computer Vision, ed. Patrick Henry Winston (New York: McGraw Hill, 1975), 211–77.

16. For more on the pragmatics of interaction, see Sigurd D'hondt, Jan-Ola Östman, and Jef Verschueren, eds., *The Pragmatics of Interaction* (Amsterdam and Philadelphia: John Benjamins, 2009).

17. For more on nonverbal frames, see Jürgen Streeck, Charles Goodwin, and Curtis LeBaron, eds., *Embodied Interaction: Language and Body in the Material World* (Cambridge: Cambridge University Press, 2011).

18. See more about language and environment in P. Auer and J. E. Schmidt, *Language and Space: An International Handbook of Linguistic Variation* (Berlin: Walter de Gruyter, 2010). For a discussion of ecologies of technology, see

B. A. Nardi and V. O'Day, *Information Ecologies: Using Technology with Heart* (Cambridge, MA: MIT Press, 1999).

19. Nick Confalone, "Can You Name the Basic Joke Structure That's Used in 'The Office,' 'Horrible Bosses,' 'Parks and Recreation,' etc.," accessed December 8, 2015, https://www.quora.com/Can-you-name-the-basic-joke-structure-thats-used-in-The-Office-Horrible-Bosses-Parks-and-Recreation-etc.

20. For work on subgroups in global teams, see M. B. O'Leary and M. Mortenson, "Friends and Enemies Within: The Roles of Subgroups, Imbalance, and Isolates in Geographically Dispersed Teams," *Organization Science* 21 (201): 115–31; and N. Panteli and R. M. Davison, "The Role of Subgroups in the Communication Patterns of Global Virtual Teams," *IEEE Transactions on Professional Communication* 18 (2005): 191–200.

21. Muriel Saville-Troike, *The Ethnography of Communication: An Introduction* (Oxford: Wiley, 2008), 127.

22. A. Y. Lewin M. Peacock, C. Peeters, J. Russell, and G. Sutton, *Duke University CIBER/Archstone Consulting 2nd Bi-Annual Offshore Survey Results* (Durham, NC: Duke CIBER/Archstone Consulting, 2005).

23. Richard Metters. "A Case Study of National Culture and Offshoring Services," *International Journal of Operations & Production Management* 28, no. 8 (2008): 727–47.

24. See also Martha L. Maznevski and Katherine M. Chudoba, "Bridging Space over Time: Global Virtual Team Dynamics and Effectiveness," *Organization Science* 11, no. 5 (September/October 2000): 473–92.

25. Suzanne Dikker, Lauren J. Silbert, Uri Hasson, and Jason D. Zevin, "On the Same Wavelength: Predictable Language Enhances Speaker–Listener Brain-to-Brain Synchrony in Posterior Superior Temporal Gyrus," *Journal of Neuroscience* 34, no. 18 (April 2014): 6267–72.

26. A. Pomerantz, "Agreeing and Disagreeing with Assessments: Some Features of Preferred/Dispreferred Turn Shapes," in *Structures of Social Action*, ed. J. M. Atkinson and J. Heritage (Cambridge: Cambridge University Press, 1984), 57–101.

27. From Herbert H. Clark and Susan E. Brennan, "Grounding in Communication," in *Readings in Groupware and Computer-Supported Cooperative Work: Assisting Human–Human Collaboration*, ed. Ronald M. Baecker (San Francisco: Morgan Kaufmann, 1993).

28. George Lakoff and Mark Johnson, *Metaphors We Live By* (Chicago: University of Chicago Press, 1980).

29. Lucy Suchman, "Technologies of Accountability: Of Lizards and Aeroplanes," in *Technology in Working Order: Studies of Work, Interaction and Technology*, ed. Graham Button (London: Routledge, 1992), 113–26.

30. Margaret Murphy and Mike Levy, "Politeness in Intercultural Email Communication: Australian and Korean Perspectives," *Journal of Intercultural Communication* 12 (2006): 1404–34.

31. English speakers are said to rely more on tact than deference in politeness practices; see G. N. Leech, *Principles of Pragmatics* (London: Longman, 1983), 107.

32. Marina Jirotka, Nigel Gilbert, and Paul Luff, "On the Social Organisation of Organisations," *Computer Supported Cooperative Work* 1, nos. 1–2 (1992): 95–118.

33. For a view of different team structures, see Bradley L. Kirkman, Benson Rosen, Paul E. Tesluk, and Cristina B. Gibson, "The Impact of Team Empowerment on Virtual Team Performance: The Moderating Role of Face-to-Face Interaction," *Academy of Management Journal* 47, no. 2 (April 2004): 175–92. Also see J. E. Hoch and S. W. J. Kozlowski, "Leading Virtual Teams: Hierarchical Leadership, Structural Supports, and Shared Team Leadership," *Journal of Applied Psychology* 99, no. 3 (2014): 390–403.

34. See John Gumperz, *Discourse Strategies* (Cambridge: Cambridge University Press, 1982), 65.

35. Michael Tomasello, *The Cultural Origins of Human Cognition* (Cambridge, MA: Harvard University Press, 1999).

5. LANGUAGE IS SOCIAL (AND CULTURAL)

1. For work on language in Silicon Valley, see Bonnie McElhinny, "Silicon Valley Sociolinguistics? Analyzing Language, Gender, and *Communities of Practice* in the New Knowledge Economy," in *Language in Late Capitalism: Pride and Profit*, ed. Alexandre Duchêne and Monica Heller (New York: Routledge, 2012), 230–60.

2. Dino Grandoni, "Mastermind Behind BuzzFeed's Quizzes Explains How They Work and Why They're So Crazy Viral," *Huffington Post*, February 24, 2014, http://www.huffingtonpost.com/2014/02/20/buzzfeed-quiz-how-do-they-work_n_4810992.html.

3. Whereas to Hindus, an overemphasis on the self has harmful consequences for the self.

4. There's a Latina version of *Cosmopolitan* designed to reflect differences in the Latina idea of the person. See Geneva Gámez-Vallejo, "Cosmopolitan for Latinas: A Call for Latina Fashionistas, Businesswomen and Beauty Insiders," *San Diego La Prensa*, May 4, 2012, http://laprensa-sandiego.org/featured/cosmopolitan-for-latinas-a-call-for-latina-fashionistas-businesswomen-and-beauty-insiders/.

5. S. Anandalakshmy, *Cultural Themes in the Indian Context* (New Delhi: Indian Council for Social Science Research, 1986).

6. N. Chaudhary, "Persistent Patterns in Cultural Negotiations of the Self: Using Dialogical Self Theory to Understand Self–Other Dynamics within Culture," *International Journal for Dialogical Science* 3, no. 1 (2008): 9–30.

7. S. O. Hastings, "Self-Disclosure and Identity Management by Bereaved Parents," *Communication Studies* 51 (2000): 352–71.

8. Chaudhary, "Persistent Patterns in Cultural Negotiations."

9. John Ogbu, *Minority Education and Caste: The American System in Cross-Cultural Perspective* (San Diego: Academic Press, 1978). For interesting language issues, see also Ben Rampton, *Crossing: Language and Ethnicity among Adolescents* (London: Longman, 1995). See also Shalini Shankar, *Desi Land: Teen Culture, Class, and Success in Silicon Valley* (Durham, NC: Duke University Press, 2008); and Jennifer Reynolds and Elaine Chun, eds., "Figuring Citizenship: Communicative Practices Mediating the Cultural Politics of Citizenship and Age," special issue, *Language & Communication* 33 (2013).

10. Clyde Kluckhohn, *Mirror for Man* (New York: Fawcett, 1949).

11. G. Hofstede, "Dimensionalizing Cultures: The Hofstede Model in Context," *Online Readings in Psychology and Culture* 2, no. 1 (2011), http://dx.doi.org/10.9707/2307-0919.1014.

12. Hofstede's power distance calculation refers to whether members of a society accept and expect that power is distributed unequally, or whether they question authority and attempt to redistribute power.

13. Penelope Brown and Stephen Levinson, *Politeness* (Cambridge: Cambridge University Press, 1987); and Erving Goffman, *Interaction Ritual: Essays on Face-to-Face Behavior* (Garden City, NY: Anchor Books, 1967).

14. See Alessandro Duranti, "Universal and Culture-Specific Properties of Greetings," *Journal of Linguistic Anthropology* 7 (1997): 63–97.

15. In Japan this is also the case.

16. Susan Herring, "Posting in a Different Voice: Gender and Ethics in Computer-Mediated Communication," in *Computer Media and Communication: A Reader*, ed. P. A. Mayer (New York: Oxford University Press, 1999), 241–65.

17. In some cultures, though, abrupt phone-call endings are fine.

18. Erving Goffman, *Interaction Ritual: Essays on Face-to-Face Behavior* (New York: Anchor Books, 1967).

19. Penelope Brown and Stephen C. Levinson, *Politeness: Some Universals in Language Usage* (Cambridge: Cambridge University Press, 1987).

20. Yanrong Chang, "You Think I Am Stupid? Face Needs in Intercultural Conflicts," *Journal of Intercultural Communication* 25 (March 2011): 4.

21. Stella Ting-Toomey, "The Matrix of Face: An Updated Face-Negotiation Theory," in *Theorizing about Intercultural Communication*, ed. William B. Gudykunst (Thousand Oaks, CA: Sage, 2005), pp. 71–92.

22. R. Singh, "Explorations in the Ethnography of Discourse," in *The Proceedings of the 1983 CASA Conference*, ed. S. Pendakur (Vancouver: University of British Columbia, 1983): 35–41.

23. Singh, "Explorations in the Ethnography of Discourse."

24. For more on this, see Barbara Johnstone, "Indexing the Local," in *Handbook of Language and Globalization*, ed. Nikolas Coupland (Oxford: Oxford University Press, 2010), 386–405; and D. S. Ellis, "Speech and Social Status in America," *Social Forces* 45 (1967): 431–37.

25. E. B. Ryan, and R. J. Sebastian, "The Effects of Speech Style and Social Class Background on Social Judgments of Speakers," *British Journal of Social and Clinical Psychology* 19 (1980): 229–33.

26. For an interesting discussion of this, see Michael Silverstein, "Indexical Order and the Dialectics of Sociolinguistic Life," *Language & Communication* 23, nos. 3–4 (July–October 2003): 193–229; and Charles Peirce, *The Writings of Charles S. Peirce: A Chronological Edition*, vols. 1–6, 8 (Bloomington: Indiana University Press, 1982).

27. For discussions of identities in such settings, see John Heritage and Steve Clayman. *Talk in Action: Interactions, Identities, and Institutions* (Malden, MA: Wiley Blackwell, 2010); also see Scott F. Kiesling, "Dude," *American Speech* 79, no. 3 (2004): 281–305.

28. Ruchir Joshi, "Broken and Spoken: On the Varieties of English Speech in South Asia," *Telegraph* (Calcutta), March 21, 2011; see also Chaise La Dousa, *Hindi Is Our Ground, English Is Our Sky* (New York: Berghahn, 2014).

29. See the work of Frederik Barth on the importance of those factors people themselves find significant in terms of identity, such as ethnicity; Frederick Barth, *Ethnic Groups and Boundaries: The Social Organization of Culture Difference* (London: Allen and Unwin, 1969). See also Michael Agar, *Language Shock: Understanding the Culture of Conversation* (Cambridge: Cambridge University Press, 1994).

30. Charles Goodwin and Marjorie Goodwin, "Assessments and the Construction of Context," in *Rethinking Context: Language as an Interactive Phenomenon*, ed. Alessandro Duranti and Charles Goodwin (Cambridge: Cambridge University Press, 1992), 147–90. See also Anna Lindström and Lorenza Mondada, "Assessments in Social Interaction: Introduction to the Special Issue," *Research on Language and Social Interaction* 42, no. 4 (2009): 299–308.

31. Roland Barthes, *Elements of Semiology* (New York: Hill and Wang, 1967), 9–34.

CONCLUSION

1. See, for example, G. Stahl, M. Maznevski, A. Voigt, and K. Jonsen, "Unraveling the Effects of Cultural Diversity in Teams: A Meta-Analysis of Research on Multicultural Work Groups," *Journal of International Business Studies* 41, no. 4 (2009): 690–709, where gains in creativity and satisfaction are

found. Also see M. Maloney and M. Zellmer-Bruhn, "Building Bridges, Windows and Cultures: Mediating Mechanisms between Team Heterogeneity and Performance in Global Teams," *Management International Review* 46, no. 6 (2006): 697–720.

2. For a discussion of a virtual R & D team, see Manju K. Ahuja, Dennis F. Galletta, and Kathleen M. Carley, "Individual Centrality and Performance in Virtual R&D Groups: An Empirical Study," *Management Science* 49, no. 1 (January 2003): 21–38; and Frank Siebdrat, Martin Hoegl, and Holger Ernst, "How to Manage Virtual Teams," *MIT Sloan Management Review* 50 (2009): 63–68.

3. See also discussions in P. W. Vlaar, P. C. Van Fenema, and V. Tiwari, "Cocreating Understanding and Value in Distributed Work: How Members of Onsite and Offshore Vendor Teams Give, Make, Demand, and Break Sense," *MIS Quarterly* 32 (2008): 227–55. And see Timothy R. Kayworth and Dorothy E. Leidner, "Leadership Effectiveness in Global Virtual Teams," *Journal of Management Information Systems* 18, no. 3 (Winter 2001/02): 7–40, for a discussion of leadership skills.

Index

action: initiating and responding, 65–66, 154; language as, 10, 19–20, 49–50, 54–74, 151, 154; power relations and, 68–72; with respect, 60, 73; "we" actions, 61–62

Africa: Dinka people and cattle color, 44; granary collapse, 158n9; parents, 89; Tortoise joke, 100–101, 105, 106

African-American culture, hearers, 80

ambiguity, 10, 25, 80; hearer and, 22, 60–61, 90–99, 152; intentional, 56; repairing common ground, 114; requests, 155–56. *See also* indirectness

Americans: *Dallas*, 84, 129; directives, 29–30, 59; idioms, 47–48; indirectness, 30, 91–92; information-transfer model of communication, 32–33; information value, 37; language actions, 49; metaphors, 46–47; peer-to-peer relations, 22; and Queen's English, 35; speaker-centric communication, 36; speech acts, 55; thank-you's, 142–43. *See also* Brazilian and American communications; Indian and American communications; Romanian and American communications

Andaman Islanders, 44

anthropology, linguistic, 11, 16

Aristotle, 77–78

assumptions about communication, 18–24, 109, 152–54; background information, 18, 21, 33, 38, 121, 125, 153; common ground, 113, 124; "culture neutral," 19, 41–43, 153; in hearing feedback, 97; how much information, 19, 38, 153; information is all the same, 19, 36–37, 152; information-transfer model of communication, 18, 20, 25, 28–33, 118, 152; myth of universal hearer, 18, 33–36, 84–87; about pausing, 113; purpose of communication, 18, 20; rules of communication, 19, 39–41; speaking the same language, 19, 34–35, 152–53. *See also* direct and clear communication; misunderstandings

Australians, common ground, 122, 123

autonomy: directives and, 30, 58, 60, 90; knowing personal history and, 88; requests and, 155–56; rules and, 41; theory of the person and, 134, 139–43

Bacall, Lauren, 86

background information: assumptions, 18, 21, 33, 38, 121, 125, 153; common-ground building, 21, 51, 121, 123, 125; jokes, 104–12

Beowulf, 54, 163n1